plurall

Parabéns!
Agora você faz parte do **Plurall**, a plataforma digital do seu livro didático!
Acesse e conheça todos os recursos e funcionalidades disponíveis para as suas aulas digitais.

Baixe o aplicativo do **Plurall** para Android e IOS ou acesse **www.plurall.net** e cadastre-se utilizando o seu código de acesso exclusivo:

CB027826

AAAHTR7SQ

Este é o seu código de acesso Plurall.
Cadastre-se e ative-o para ter acesso aos conteúdos relacionados a esta obra.

@plurallnet

@plurallnetoficial

SOMOS
EDUCAÇÃO

ELIETE CANESI MORINO

Graduada pela Pontifícia Universidade Católica de São Paulo em Língua e Literatura Inglesas e Tradução e Interpretação.

Especialização em Língua Inglesa pela International Bell School of London.

Pós-graduada em Metodologia da Língua Inglesa pela Faculdade de Tecnologia e Ciência.

Atuou como professora da rede particular de ensino e em projetos comunitários.

RITA BRUGIN DE FARIA

Graduada pela Faculdade de Arte Santa Marcelina e pela Faculdade Paulista de Artes.

Especialização em Língua Inglesa pela International Bell School of London.

Pós-graduada em Metodologia da Língua Inglesa pela Faculdade de Tecnologia e Ciência.

Especialista em alfabetização, atuou como professora e coordenadora pedagógica das redes pública e particular de ensino.

teens

Hello!

8 STAGE

ea
editora ática

editora ática

Direção Presidência: Mario Ghio Júnior

Direção de Conteúdo e Operações: Wilson Troque

Direção editorial: Luiz Tonolli e Lidiane Vivaldini Olo

Gestão de projeto editorial: Mirian Senra

Gestão de área: Alice Silvestre

Coordenação: Renato Malkov

Edição: Ana Lucia Militello, Carla Fernanda Nascimento (assist.), Caroline Santos, Danuza Dias Gonçalves, Maiza Prande Bernardello, Milena Rocha (assist.), Sabrina Cairo Bileski

Planejamento e controle de produção: Patrícia Eiras e Adjane Queiroz

Revisão: Hélia de Jesus Gonsaga (ger.), Kátia Scaff Marques (coord.), Rosângela Muricy (coord.), Ana Curci, Ana Paula C. Malfa, Arali Gomes, Brenda T. M. Morais, Diego Carbone, Gabriela M. Andrade, Luís M. Boa Nova, Patricia Cordeiro, Paula T. de Jesus, Ricardo Miyake; Amanda T. Silva e Bárbara de M. Genereze (estagiárias)

Arte: Daniela Amaral (ger.), Catherine Saori Ishihara (coord.) e Letícia Lavôr (edit. arte)

Diagramação: Estúdio Lima

Iconografia e tratamento de imagem: Sílvio Kligin (ger.), Claudia Bertolazzi (coord.), Mariana Valeiro (pesquisa iconográfica), Cesar Wolf e Fernanda Crevin (tratamento)

Licenciamento de conteúdos de terceiros: Thiago Fontana (coord.), Flavia Zambon e Angra Marques (licenciamento de textos), Erika Ramires, Luciana Pedrosa Bierbauer, Luciana Cardoso Sousa e Claudia Rodrigues (analistas adm.)

Ilustrações: Filipe Rocha, Henrique Heráclio, Nik Neves e Olavo Costa

Cartografia: Eric Fuzii (coord.), Robson Rosendo da Rocha (edit. arte)

Design: Gláucia Koller (ger.), Talita Guedes (proj. gráfico e capa) e Gustavo Vanini (assist. arte)

Foto de capa: Yukmin/Asia Images/Getty Images

Dados Internacionais de Catalogação na Publicação (CIP)

```
Morino, Eliete Canesi
   Hello teens 8º ano / Eliete Canesi Morino, Rita Brugin
de Faria. - 8. ed. - São Paulo : Ática, 2019.

   Suplementado pelo manual do professor.
   Bibliografia.
   ISBN: 978-85-08-19354-7 (aluno)
   ISBN: 978-85-08-19355-4 (professor)


   1.   Língua inglesa (Ensino fundamental). I. Faria,
Rita Brugin de. II. Título.


2019-0179                         CDD: 372.652
```

Julia do Nascimento - Bibliotecária - CRB-8/010142

2024
Código da obra 885258
OP: 251061 (AL)
1ª impressão
1ª edição
De acordo com a BNCC.

Impressão acabamento: EGB Editora Gráfica Bernardi

Uma publicação

WELCOME, STUDENTS, TO HELLO! TEENS 8

Hello!

A língua inglesa está cada vez mais presente no nosso dia a dia. Ela chega até nós por intermédio dos mais diversos canais de comunicação e, assim, a todo momento estamos ouvindo, lendo e falando espontaneamente em inglês.

Em virtude da evolução da tecnologia, as distâncias tornaram-se virtuais e o inglês é o idioma mais utilizado por pessoas de diferentes nacionalidades que querem se comunicar entre si.

A **Coleção Hello! Teens**, escrita para você, um adolescente do mundo contemporâneo, quer motivá-lo a aprender inglês por meio de temas instigantes associados a atividades que facilitarão sua aprendizagem.

Participe ativamente das aulas refletindo e interagindo com seus colegas e desfrute de todos os benefícios que esta aprendizagem pode lhe proporcionar!

As autoras

CONTENTS

WELCOME!

1 Look at the picture and read the text. Then match the columns.

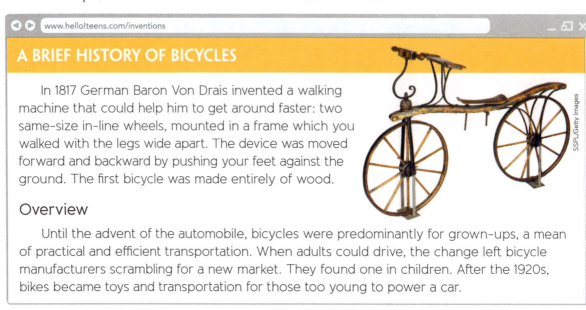

www.hello!teens.com/inventions

A BRIEF HISTORY OF BICYCLES

In 1817 German Baron Von Drais invented a walking machine that could help him to get around faster: two same-size in-line wheels, mounted in a frame which you walked with the legs wide apart. The device was moved forward and backward by pushing your feet against the ground. The first bicycle was made entirely of wood.

SSPL/Getty Images

Overview

Until the advent of the automobile, bicycles were predominantly for grown-ups, a mean of practical and efficient transportation. When adults could drive, the change left bicycle manufacturers scrambling for a new market. They found one in children. After the 1920s, bikes became toys and transportation for those too young to power a car.

Based on: <https://www.sportsrec.com/357076-the-history-of-the-bicycle-for-kids.html#ixzz1h0lgWkdJ>.
Accessed on: Feb. 25, 2019.

a. to get around   ◯ a great distance away

b. same-size in-line wheels   ◯ an adult

c. wide apart   ◯ to go to a lot of places

d. device   ◯ a hurried attempt to get something

e. grown-up   ◯ similar size wheels in a straight line

f. scrambling for   ◯ a machine or object made for a particular
                purpose; an invention, especially a
                mechanical or electrical one

2 Answer the questions according to the text in activity 1.

a. What did Baron Von Drais invent? Why did he do it?

_____

b. Before the invention of the automobile, were bicycles exclusively a mean of transportation?

_____

c. What happened to the bicycle after the 1920s?

_____

3 Find in the text in activity 1 eight verbs in the Simple Past and write them in the appropriate column.

Regular		Irregular	

4 Look at the famous Georges-Pierre Seurat's painting and answer the questions.

Reprodução/Instituto de Arte de Chicago, Chicago, EUA.

A Sunday Afternoon on the Island of La Grande Jatte – 1884-1886, oil on canvas, 207.5 cm x 308.1 cm.

a. Does the painting represent a scene from the present or the past? What elements in the painting help you reach this conclusion?

_____

b. What period of the day did the painter represent?

_____

c. How do you feel when you look at the painting?

_____

5 Look at the painting again and check the elements you can see in it.

◯ children	◯ a black dog	◯ a river	◯ women
◯ birds	◯ flowers	◯ houses	◯ men
◯ a monkey	◯ a cat	◯ trees	◯ grass
◯ boats	◯ a bicycle	◯ umbrellas	◯ a ball

6 Answer the questions about the painting in activity 4.

a. Where are these people? What are they doing?

_____

b. What are the predominant colors in the painting?

_____

c. Are there any boats represented in the picture?

_____

d. In your opinion, why are some people looking at the river?

_____

7 Now, read a text about the painting and the artist who made it.

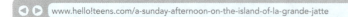 www.hello!teens.com/a-sunday-afternoon-on-the-island-of-la-grande-jatte

Georges Seurat's spent two years (1884-1886) painting *A Sunday Afternoon on the Island of La Grande Jatte*, in which tiny dots of multi-colored paint (pointillism technique) on the 10ft canvas appear to blend into solid colors. As a painter, Georges-Pierre Seurat wanted to make a difference and with *La Grand Jatte*, he succeeded.

A Sunday Afternoon on the Island of La Grande Jatte is both the best-known and largest painting Georges Seurat ever created on a canvas. It depicts people relaxing in a suburban park on an island in the Seine River called La Grande Jatte, a popular retreat for the middle and upper class of Paris in the 19th century. This iconic painting is now regarded as part of our culture and as one of the most pivotal works of art ever put onto a canvas.

Nowadays, it can be viewed at the Art Institute of Chicago.

TO LEARN MORE

Watch the video "Get to the point: Georges Seurat and Pointillism". Available at: <https://www.youtube.com/watch?v=R9DX5MhkfYQ>. Accessed on: Feb. 25, 2019.

8 Complete the sentences using **can**, **could**, **can't** or **couldn't**.

a. Mary _____ swim very well. She can swim every day because it's summer.

b. There are so many different flowers in spring; I _____ decide which one to choose.

c. The children _____ play outside, because it started to rain.

d. I _____ sleep last night because it was so hot!

e. _____ you lend me an eraser, please?

9 Look at the pictures and answer: What is the weather like?

It's _____. It's _____. It's _____.

It's _____. It's _____. It's _____.

10 Match the words to the pictures and role-play with a classmate. Are you ready to order? Take notes.

FOOD TRUCK MENU

APPETIZERS
1. TOSSED SALAD
2. TOMATO SOUP

MAIN COURSE
3. STEAK AND VEGETABLES
4. SPAGHETTI AND MEATBALLS
5. FISH AND CHIPS

DESSERTS
6. ICE CREAM
7. APPLE PIE

SANDWICHES
8. VEGETARIAN SANDWICH
9. CHEESEBURGER

BEVERAGES
10. ORANGE JUICE
11. ICED TEA
12. SODA

Olavo Costal
Arquivo da editora

potowizard/Shutterstock

1 Look at the picture and discuss with your classmates.

    a. Why is it important to learn English?

    b. In what countries is the English language spoken? Do you think it is spoken the same way?

2 Read and listen to the dialog. Then act out.

Kitty: Hi, Leo!

Leo: Hi, Kitty! Check it out! I'm watching a documentary on TV.

Kitty: What is it about?

Leo: It's about life in Australia. There were interviews with some people from Sydney. There was a man eating Australian traditional food too. Now they are talking about their culture.

Kitty: Listen! They use different words and expressions in English.

Leo: Yes, I know! They say "barbie" for barbecue; "arvo" for afternoon, and "mozzies" for mosquitos.

Kitty: That's really cool!

Leo: Also, they speak with a different accent from ours.

Reporter: That's it! Good on ya!

Kitty: What is he saying?

Leo: He is saying "well done"!

Kitty: That sounds so different.

Leo: Yes, but it's just a different accent from the one we know. In other English-speaking countries there are words spelled and pronounced differently as well. It's always fun to learn more, isn't it?

3 Answer the questions according to the dialog.

    a. How do Australians say barbecue, mosquitos and afternoon?

    _____

    b. Why do you think these words are different in Australia?

    _____

1 Read the cartoon and answer the questions.

©Yves Cotten/Acervo do cartunista

a. What is this cartoon about?

_____

b. What scene shows a simplified form of English?

_____

c. In the first scene, what is the man's intention in asking such a long question?

_____

d. Can a non-native speaker of English understand the second picture?

_____

2 There are many ways of expressing yourself in English, one of them is using Globish. Read the quote and answer **T** (true) or **F** (false).

Andriy M/Shutterstock

> Globish is English, is even meant to be very correct English, but it is what we call English light, a simplified form of English, with less words, you go with 1600 to 1500 words.
>
> Jean Paul Nerriére

a. ◯ Globish is an incorrect use of the English language.

b. ◯ Globish is a very sophisticated and formal language.

c. ◯ Globish allows you to communicate in English using about 1500 words.

d. ◯ Globish allows you to use standard grammatical structures as it is a simple language.

WORD WORK

1 Listen and repeat the words. 🔊3

🇺🇸 theater
🇬🇧 theatre

🇺🇸🇦🇺 stove
🇬🇧 cooker

🇺🇸 soccer
🇬🇧 football

🇺🇸🇦🇺 can
🇬🇧 tin

🇺🇸 cookies
🇬🇧🇦🇺 biscuits

🇺🇸 candy bar
🇨🇦 chocolate bar

🇺🇸 elevator
🇬🇧🇦🇺 lift

🇺🇸🇦🇺 truck
🇬🇧 lorry

🇺🇸 apartment
🇬🇧 flat

🇺🇸🇦🇺 sick
🇬🇧 ill

🇺🇸 faucet
🇬🇧🇨🇦 tap

🇺🇸 meatballs
🇿🇦 frikkadels

2 Match the North American words to their British variants.

North American English

a. garbage
b. mark
c. gas
d. mail
e. color
f. eraser
g. pants
h. subway
i. movies
j. French fries

British English

○ colour
○ rubbish
○ trousers
○ chips
○ petrol
○ grade
○ rubber
○ cinema
○ underground
○ post

3 Read the British words and do some research for the North American equivalent.

	British	North American
	fizzy drink	
	torch	
	taxi	
	trainers	
	headmaster	

	British	North American
	car park	
	shop	
	pavement	
	toilet	
	mobile phone	

Let's play **Sausage Game** and **Word List**!

Banco de imagens/Arquivo da editora

Ilustrações: Olavo Costa/Arquivo da editora

FOCUS ON LANGUAGE

1 Read the cartoon and check the correct sentence.

   ◯ In the cartoon, "I was a glass of water" is in the present.

   ◯ In the cartoon, "I was a glass of water" is in the past.

   ◯ There is a sentence with the verb to be in the negative form.

"My psychic tells me I was a glass of water in a previous life."

2 Read and complete the chart.

Verb to be – Simple Past								
Affirmative			**Interrogative**			**Negative**		
I	was	in the US.	Was	I	in the US?	I		in the US.
You	were	in China.		you	in China?	You	weren't (were not)	in China.
He She It	was	in the park.		he she it	in the park?	He She It	wasn't (was not)	in the park.
We You They		at home.	Were	we you they	at home?	We You they		at home.

3 Write the name of the places where these people were last weekend.

  a. The tourists _____.

  b. Tracy _____ with her friends.

  c. The students _____.

GRAMMAR
HELPER

Go to page 167.

4 Read the dialog and pay attention to the verbs in blue. Then check.

> **Leo:** Hi, Kitty! What were you doing in the morning?
>
> **Kitty:** I was studying Math at Carol's house.

a. ( ) The main structure is: *verb to be in the past + main verb + ing.*

b. ( ) The main structure is: *verb to be in the present + main verb + ing.*

5 Read the chart, unscramble the words and write sentences using the Past Continuous.

Past Continuous								
Affirmative			**Negative**			**Interrogative**		
I	was	working yesterday.	I	wasn't	working yesterday.	Was	I	working yesterday?
You	were		You	weren't		Were	you	
He/She	was		He/She	wasn't		Was	he/she	
We You They	were		We You They	weren't		Were	we you they	

eat

the

the   to   Jamaican   Allan   study

listen   restaurant

music   tourists   in   Spanish   students

a

a. _____   b. _____   c. _____

_____   _____   _____

6 Read the cartoon and underline the correct alternatives.

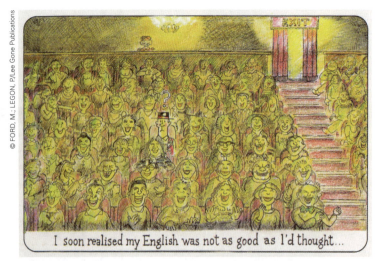

I soon realised my English was not as good as I'd thought...

FORD, M.; LEGON, P. *The How to Be British Collection.* Brighton: Lee Gone Publications, 2006. p. 11.

a. They (were/was) at the movie theater.

b. Why (was/were) they laughing? Because the movie (were/was) funny.

c. The foreign man among the people (weren't/wasn't) laughing because he could not understand the movie.

GRAMMAR HELPER

Go to page 168.

7 Look at Jim's and Kitty's schedules from yesterday. What were they doing...

Jim

8:00 a.m. – go to school

12:30 p.m. – go home

1:00 p.m. – have lunch

2:00 p.m. – go to Spanish class

4:00 p.m. – do my homework

5:30 p.m. – go to my grandmother's house

7:00 p.m. – wash the dishes

Kitty

8:00 a.m. – go to school

12:30 p.m. – go home

1:00 p.m. – have lunch

2:00 p.m. – go to the dentist

4:00 p.m. – do my homework

5:30 p.m. – study Math

7:00 p.m – walk Fido

Ilustrações: Filipe Rocha/Arquivo da editora

a. at 8:00 a.m.?

They were going to school.

b. at 12:30 p.m.? _____

c. at 1:00 p.m.? _____

d. at 2:00 p.m.? _____

e. at 4:00 p.m.? _____

f. at 5:30 p.m.? _____

g. at 7:00 p.m.? _____

8 How about you? What were you doing at 7:00 p.m. yesterday?

_____

9 Read this fragment from the opening dialog. Leo describes the documentary he was watching. Then write **T** (true) or **F** (false).

> **Leo:** It's about life in Australia. There were interviews with some people from Sydney. There was a man eating Australian traditional food too. Now they are talking about their culture.

a. ◯ In the sentence "Now they are talking about their culture", the verb to be is in the past tense.

b. ◯ "There were" is used in a plural sentence and "there was", in a singular one.

c. ◯ The words in blue indicate that something existed or happened in the past.

10 Read the chart and complete the dialog using the past form of there to be.

There to be – Simple Past								
Affirmative			**Negative**			**Interrogative**		
There	was	a test at school yesterday.	There	wasn't	a test at school yesterday.	Was	there	a test at school yesterday?
There	were	tests at school yesterday.	There	weren't	tests at school yesterday.	Were	there	tests at school yesterday?

Samuel: Where were you last weekend?

Martin: I was at the beach with my parents. The weather was great and _____ many people there.

Samuel: _____ any events happening?

Martin: Yes, _____ a surf championship.

Samuel: That's awesome!

Martin: Yes, _____ many surfers from different parts of the country.

Samuel: And _____ a prize for the winner?

Martin: Yes, the champion won a trip to Hawaii.

Samuel: Wow! What a prize!

Go to page 168.

Monkey Business Images /Shutterstock

LISTEN AND SPEAK

1 You are going to listen to some people with different accents talking in English. First, look at the flags below and write what countries they are from.

_____

2 Now, listen to different accents and number the flags.

a.  ☐   b.  ☐   c.  ☐   d.  ☐

Bandeiras: Banco de imagens/ Arquivo da editora

3 Now listen to *A Reggae Song* and complete the lyrics.

A Reggae Song

A Jamaican inspiration,

Let me create a new _____.
It takes some imagination,

This rhythm is nice and _____.
Bass and keyboard,
Guitar, horn, sax and drums.

This _____ is really upbeat,
It's quick and exciting indeed.

Reggae is made for _____.

Feel the rhythm and bend your knees,
Run around all the place,

Left foot, right hand, _____ the beat.

The words, I cannot _____,
Jamaican Talk, oh, no way.
"Mi a-go lef today"
Is the same as
"I'm leaving today".
Oh, oh, oh...
I said today.
Oh, oh, oh...

This song was especially composed for this book. ISRC BR–LAW–09–00015.

David Buzzard / Alamy/Fotoarena

4 Find in the lyrics a Jamaican expression. What does it mean?

_____

5 In pairs, do some research about English spelling and vocabulary varieties and do an oral presentation to your classmates.

These expressions can be useful:

• How do you say... in England/Canada/New Zealand?

• In Scotland, they say…

PRONUNCIATION
CORNER

1 Listen to the jazz chant and act out.
6

Nik Neves/Arquivo da editora

That's Ms. High.
Ms. High? Really?
Does she have a tie on her thigh?
Yes, she has a tie on her thigh!
Oh! A tie on her thigh!
Unbelievable!

Matt's bat is back and black.
The math teacher Matt has a bat?!!!

Yes, and it needs a bath.
A bath or a rest?
A bath, not a rest.

There are three bees in the tree.
Is it true?
Yes, it is true.
The three trees have bees.
Can't you see through?

2 Write the words in the correct columns according to their sounds.
7

| together | there | then | Cynthia | think |
| thought | truth | both | seventh | they |

Voiced /ð/	Voiceless /θ/

3 Challenge a classmate: In pairs, ask other words that have the sounds studied in activity 2. They must be part of different categories: a cardinal number, an ordinal number, a noun, an adjective, a school subject etc.

READ AND WRITE

1 Scan the feature article and complete the sentences below.

a. _____ published the article.

b. The date of the article is _____

c. _____ wrote the article.

d. _____ is the title of the article.

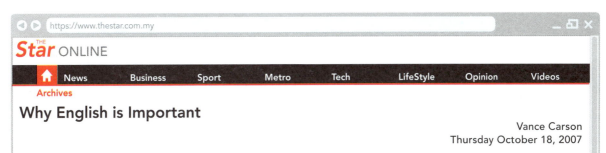

https://www.thestar.com.my

Star THE ONLINE

| Home | News | Business | Sport | Metro | Tech | LifeStyle | Opinion | Videos |

Archives

Why English is Important

Vance Carson
Thursday October 18, 2007

If you are currently learning English in a school, college or institute of further education, you join approximately one billion other people around the world who are engaged in the same pursuit. However, as you try to memorise proper grammar, and try to avoid the mistakes common to most students of English, you may wonder why you are learning the language in the first place [...]

After Mandarin, English is spoken by more people than any other language, and is the native language of more than 350 million people. More people speak English than those who speak the Arabic and French languages combined.

Moreover, English is the international language of diplomacy, business, science, technology, banking, computing, medicine, aviation, [...] armed forces, engineering, [...] tourism, films and arguably the best pop and rock music in the world.

English has plenty of words to choose from. In fact, an English speaker is offered the biggest vocabulary of any language with a choice of 500,000 to 1,000,000 words (including technical and scientific terms).

But don't panic, most English speakers do very well with a vocabulary of around 20,000 words.

English can be fun too. For instance, the music of such stars as Elvis Presley, The Beatles, Led Zeppelin, Michael Jackson and Madonna has encouraged fans to speak the language of their idols, whilst others have enrolled in English classes to improve their understanding of the dialog in films and TV shows.

Or perhaps they have embraced English to enjoy the writing of Stephen King, George Orwell or J.K. Rowling. They may even have an interest in speaking English just to converse with travellers from other countries, who communicate by using the English global interlingua while travelling abroad.

Finally, if you are studying English at school, college or university, remember that getting an 'A' grade in English is almost worthless, in terms of communication, if you cannot speak the language. Spoken English is used in the best careers, the best universities, and is increasingly being used at job interviews. So like it or not, English is a very important language to learn how to speak.

Being able to read and write in English is not enough!

Available at: <https://www.thestar.com.my/story/?file=%2F2007%2F10%2F18%2Flifefocus%2F18963932>. Accessed on: Feb. 28, 2019.

2 Read the whole article and answer the questions.

a. What is the objective of this article?

_____

_____

_____

b. In which paragraphs can we find reasons to learn English?

_____

_____

_____

c. The article was published a long time ago. In your opinion, does it still make sense nowadays? Why?

_____

_____

_____

3 Read the fragments of the article and write **O** for opinion and **F** for fact.

a. ( ) [...] you may wonder why you are learning the language in the first place.

b. ( ) After Mandarin, English is spoken by more people than any other language.

c. ( ) [...] is the native language of more than 350 million people.

d. ( ) English can be fun too.

4 Check what we can infer from the article.

a. ( ) English is a language of international communication.

b. ( ) Spoken English is very important when it comes to communication.

c. ( ) Learning Mandarin is more important than learning English.

d. ( ) English can give you access to the world of fun and entertainment.

5 Do you agree with the author's opinions? Why (not)?

_____

_____

_____

_____

_____

_____

Text 2

6 Read the poem below. What elements can you find in it?

( ) Lines   ( ) Paragraphs   ( ) Stanzas

What Is Indian English Language?

by Bijay Kant Dubey

I know and hear about
British English, American English,
Canadian English, Australian English,
Rhodesian English, South African English
And so many varieties of it,
I mean English and Englishness,
Englishes that talk you,
But I do not know if there is a variety still
Like Indian English
And if it is, where is it spoken,
You show me the home where it is?

In a country like that of India, impregnable, full of linguistic not,
Racial and ethnic diversities not,
But natural diversities too,
So multi-ethnic, multi-racial
It was really difficult for the English to connect,
Reign and rule over
A vast tract of separated lands
And they had of a course a tough time to dispense with
And this needs to be acknowledged on our part.

[...]

Available at: <https://www.poemhunter.com/poem/what-is-indian-english-language>.
Accessed on: Feb. 15, 2019.

TO LEARN MORE

A **stanza** is one of the parts into which a poem is divided.
The **speaker** is the voice or "persona" of a poem. One should not assume that the poet is the speaker.

7 Read the statements below and check the true ones according to the poem.

a. ( ) According to the speaker, there is no variety like Indian English.

b. ( ) The speaker says that there are several religions practiced in India. That is why there is no variety like Indian English.

c. ( ) There is a great variety of English around the world and the speaker knows that.

d. ( ) The speaker says the best English is the one spoken in India.

8 Why is English important for global communication? In pairs, write a poem about it, using the ideas you discussed in class. Follow the instructions below.

a. Select useful information from Text 1 and do some research online for more.

b. Make sentences organizing this information.

c. Use these sentences to create a poem. Write a draft in your notebook.

d. Share your draft with other classmates and accept their suggestions to improve your poem.

e. Correct it with your teacher's help.

f. Write the final version on your book.

_____

_____

_____

_____

_____

_____

_____

_____

_____

_____

_____

_____

_____

_____

_____

_____

_____

9 Now, prepare a presentation. Read your poem and listen to your classmates' ones, too.

177

TIPS FOR LIFE

Cultural diversity

1 Read the cartoon and answer. What does the attitude of the cat show us?

○ happiness

○ discouragement

○ doubt

○ intolerance

2 Now, read the text and talk to a classmate. How does it relate to the cartoon in activity 1?

> In English, as well as in other languages, there is a great number of varieties and regionalisms. We have to respect these linguistic variants and try to seek the best interpretation to their meanings. Respect for linguistic variants is to recognize the diversity of the global culture.

3 Now, in groups, create a short dialog showing how two English learners from different countries understand each other and respect different accents, dialects and regionalisms.

_____

_____

_____

CHECK YOUR PROGRESS	😃	😐	🙁
English variants			
To be (Simple Past)			
Past Continuous			
There to be (Simple Past)			
Listening			
Speaking			
Reading			
Writing			

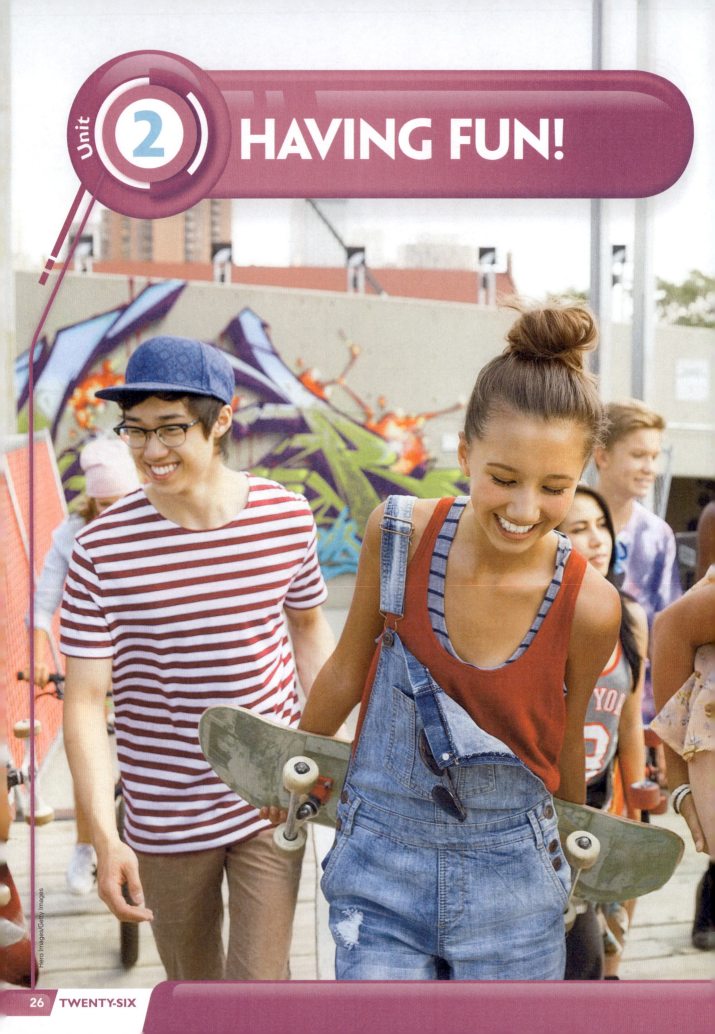

1 Look at the picture and talk to your classmates. What do you usually do to have fun?

2 Read and listen to the dialog. Then act out.

🔊8

Carol: Hi, Kitty. How was your weekend?

Kitty: Oh, it was nice!

Carol: What did you do?

Kitty: I went to my cousin's birthday party on Saturday evening.

Carol: Oh, really?

Kitty: Yeah, it was great! I danced all night and made lots of new friends.

Carol: I can imagine! You're a typical social butterfly, Kitty.

Kitty: I'm just cheerful… And I'm lazy, too! On Sunday, I watched TV all day. How about you, Carol? Did you have a nice weekend?

Carol: Yes, I did. I went to a museum with some friends on Saturday.

Kitty: How cool! Which one did you visit?

Carol: We went to MoMA! You know, I love to spend time appreciating artists and their work.

Kitty: I like to visit museums, but I prefer going to parties, where I can talk to people.

Carol: I'm the opposite… I don't feel comfortable in noisy places.

Kitty: And what about Sunday? What did you do?

Carol: My Sunday wasn't different from yours. I just listened to music and played video games.

Kitty: We are different, but not so much!

Carol: Indeed, we are!

3 Write **T** (true) or **F** (false) according to the dialog.

a. ◯ Kitty stayed at home on Sunday.

b. ◯ Carol went to a noisy party on Sunday.

c. ◯ Carol went to the museum with her family.

d. ◯ Kitty and Carol are talking about their weekend.

THINKING AHEAD

1 Read the dialog and check the correct options.

> I danced all night and made lots of new friends.

> You're a typical **social butterfly**, Kitty.

Olavo Costa/Arquivo da editora

a. According to Carol, Kitty is...

○ shy and introverted.

○ sociable and likes to be around people.

b. The expression **social butterfly** is an idiom because...

○ these words keep their individual meaning.

○ these words combined have a different meaning.

LANGUAGE TIPS

An **idiom** is a group of words whose meaning is different from the meanings of the individual words. Available at: <https://www.oxfordlearnersdictionaries.com/definition/english/idiom?q=idiom>. Accessed on: Feb. 20, 2019.

2 Read the chart. Does any of these party idioms fit your personality? Which one?

www.english-at-home.com/		
The life and soul of the party	The person who is at the center of all parties.	*Alice is the life and soul of the party.*
Let (your) hair down	Forget all your inhibitions.	*He is shy, but at parties he lets his hair down.*
A party animal	A person who loves to go to parties.	*John is a real party animal. He is never home.*
Find someone in the kitchen at parties	It refers to someone who doesn't like mixing socially.	*You will always find Kevin in the kitchen at parties.*

Available at: <www.english-at-home.com/idioms/party-idioms>. Accessed on: Feb. 20, 2019.

3 Match the columns.

a. Tina didn't talk to anyone at the party.

b. Tom is so excited today.

c. Ann is very shy at parties.

d. My brother doesn't like to socialize.

○ She needs to let her hair down.

○ At parties, you always find him in the kitchen.

○ She is a shrinking violet.

○ He is the life and soul of the party.

4 Do you know any similar expressions in Portuguese? Share them with your classmates.

1 Listen and say. Then, check the activities you like to do.

9

go to a concert

visit an art exhibition

play video game

take pictures and selfies

read a good book

walk the dog

listen to music

watch a cartoon

make a video

watch a good movie

go out with friends

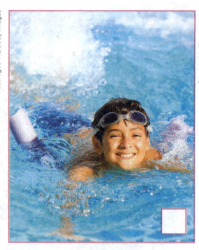

swim

practice sports

visit relatives

go to the mall

2 Complete the sentences according to your preferences.

a. I enjoy myself when I _____.

b. I like to _____ on Sundays.

c. I don't like to _____.

d. I love to _____.

e. When my friends visit me, we _____.

f. When I am sick and I stay home, I like to _____.

TIME FOR A GAME

Let's play **Hangman** and **Communicative Game**!

1 Read the comic strip and check the correct option.

a. ◯ Jon bought a jacket for Garfield, but it didn't fit.

b. ◯ Liz and Garfield had a deal to wash the jacket.

c. ◯ Garfield is happy because he can wear Jon's jacket.

GRAMMAR HELPER

Go to page 169.

2 Read the comic strip again and circle the correct options.

a. In the first panel, Jon refers to an action in the **present/past**.

b. The verb tense can be identified in the first panel by the word **washed/jacket**.

3 Read the chart and check the correct option.

Simple Past – Regular Verbs							
Affirmative		**Interrogative**			**Negative**		
I			I		I		
You			you		You		didn't (did not) play basketball yesterday.
He She	played basketball yesterday.	Did	he she	play basketball yesterday?	He She		
We You They			we you they		We You They		

Simple Past (-*ed* Rules)
1. **love** – John love**d** to meet his friend in Rome.
2. **stay** – Richard stay**ed** home all day.
3. **cry** – Lily cr**ied** a lot watching that movie yesterday.
4. **start** – Lucy start**ed** a new school last week.
5. **plan** – I plan**ned** this trip six months ago.

What is the interrogative form of the sentence "Garfield washed my jacket"?

a. ◯ Did Garfield wash my jacket?   b. ◯ Did Garfield washed my jacket?

4 Look at the pictures and complete the sentences using verbs in the Simple Past.

What did these people do last Saturday?

a. Mike _____ with his family to the beach. (travel)

_____ Mike _____ the beach? (enjoy)

No, he _____. It _____ all day long! (rain)

b. _____ Steve _____ to the sports club? (go)

No, he _____. He _____ all day at the coffee shop. (work)

c. How about you? What did you do last Saturday?

_____

_____

5 Complete the paragraph with the verbs from the box.

| watch | decide | prepare | listen | invite | play | enjoy | exchange |

Last week, Leo and his friends _____ some messages about what they did on the weekend and _____ to meet on Saturday night at Leo's house. They _____ some other friends and _____ some snacks, too. The meeting started at 6:00 p.m. They _____ video clips, _____ to music and _____ video games. They _____ the meeting and had a lot of fun.

6 Rewrite the sentences in the negative and interrogative forms.

a. Kitty danced a lot at her cousin's birthday party.

N: _____

I: _____

b. They watched a movie last weekend.

N: _____

I: _____

c. John and Liz played tennis at the sports club yesterday.

N: _____

I: _____

7 Describe the scenes using the Simple Past. What did these people do on their last vacation?

a.

kravik93/Shutterstock

_____

_____

b.

Chris Ryan/Getty Images

_____

_____

c.

Leszek Glasner/Shutterstock

_____

_____

d.

Twinsterphoto/Shutterstock

_____

_____

8 Look at the picture and write short answers to the questions.

Some of Adam's friends went to his house. They left 5 minutes ago...

a. Did Adam's friends help to clean up his place? _____

b. Did they drink all the juice from the pitcher? _____

c. Did his friends eat all the sandwiches on the table? _____

d. Did they turn off the video game before leaving? _____

	Simple Past – Short Answers	
	Affirmative	**Negative**
Did you work yesterday?	Yes, I did.	No, I didn't.

9 Rewrite the sentences replacing the words in bold with their possessive adjectives.

a. Where is **Allan's** house?

_____

b. **Kitty and Carol's** friend is a nice guy.

_____

c. I washed **Kitty's** bike yesterday.

_____

d. Do you have **Mary's** cell phone number?

_____

Personal Pronouns: I, you, he, she, it, we, you, they.
Possessive Adjectives: my, your, his, her, its, our, your, their.

LISTEN AND SPEAK

◀1 What did they do last weekend? Listen and check.
◀10

a.

 ☐

 ☐

 ☐

b.

 ☐

 ☐

 ☐

Ilustrações: Henrique Heráclio/
Arquivo da editora

◀2 Listen and check **True** or **False**.
◀11

	True	False
a. Karen didn't like the movie.		
b. William traveled to the beach last Sunday.		
c. Jane stayed home reading a book.		
d. Mary and Joseph stayed home on Saturday morning.		

IMOGI graphics /Shutterstock

Leo Drumond/Arquivo da editora

Akugasahagy/Shutterstock

Monika Buch/
Stock Photos/
Glow Images

LANGUAGE TIPS

In British English, when using the verbs **travel** and **cancel** in the Simple Past, we double the last **l** even though the last vowel is not stressed: travel – trave**lled**, cancel – cance**lled**.

3 Listen to the dialog and complete it with words from the box.

🔊12

awesome	called	cool	did	kidding
played	wanted	was	weekend	

Bart: Hey, Abbott, how was your _____?

Abbott: _____! I went to the Maroon 5 concert!

Bart: Wow! How _____ it?

Abbott: The concert was amazing! And you? What _____ you do?

Bart: Remember I told you about that event _____ PAX?

Abbott: No, _____! Did you go to that big game festival?

Bart: Yes, I did. It was _____! I _____ board and computer games.

Abbott: I really _____ to go with you. Well, maybe next time…

4 What did you do last weekend? In pairs, write a dialog and role-play it.

PRONUNCIATION CORNER

1 Listen, practice the -ed sounds and
🔊13 act out the jazz chant.

What did they do yesterday?
Jim visited his grandpa.
Kitty studied English.
Sayuri danced at a club.
Leo played a video game.
Carol listened to music.
Liz walked in the park.
Polly traveled to Miami.
John watched a cartoon.
What did John do?
John watched a cartoon.
A cartoon, at noon?
I'm sure, a cartoon at noon!

Ilustrações: Nik Neves/
Arquivo da editora

2 Listen and practice. What did they do yesterday?
🔊14 Jim visi**ted** his grandpa. Kitty stud**ied** English. Sayuri dan**ced** at the club.

Leo play**ed** video games. Carol liste**ned** to music. Liz wal**ked** in the park.

READ AND WRITE

Text 1

1 Read quickly the blog post below and answer: what kind of blog is it?

a. ◯ Fashion blog b. ◯ Business blog c. ◯ Personal blog

2 The blog belongs to Marzia Bisognin. The title of her blog post is "Hello, Ireland". What kind of information do you expect to find in it? Read the text to find out.

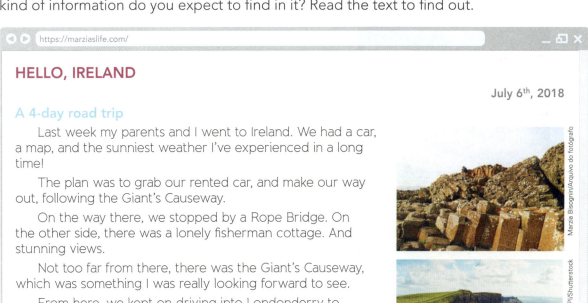

https://marziaslife.com/

HELLO, IRELAND

July 6th, 2018

A 4-day road trip

Last week my parents and I went to Ireland. We had a car, a map, and the sunniest weather I've experienced in a long time!

The plan was to grab our rented car, and make our way out, following the Giant's Causeway.

On the way there, we stopped by a Rope Bridge. On the other side, there was a lonely fisherman cottage. And stunning views.

Not too far from there, there was the Giant's Causeway, which was something I was really looking forward to see.

From here, we kept on driving into Londonderry to spend the night. We arrived quite late, and our hotel had cancelled the booking (I hadn't noticed) – which was not fun – but luckily we found a lovely boutique hotel nearby.

We woke up early, walked around the city, and then left towards Sligo. There wasn't too much to see there. After that, we went straight to Galway.

By the time we finished dinner it was 10.30 p.m., but we are lucky that the sun stays up for so long in this period, giving us some time to walk around before it gets completely dark.

City-wise, I actually think Galway was my favourite to see. It was small, but cute.

The following day we had one thing planned: The Cliffs of Moher. We took each day casually, knowing we had a destination to reach, but without stressing over what we needed to see.

But I am glad that I made sure to plan our trip around reaching these cliffs, cause they were really breathtaking.

We spent a few hours there, taking in the view and having lunch, but then we got back into the car and reached Longford, which nobody recommended visiting, but if we wanted to make it back to Belfast in time, we needed to stop by it for the night.

And so as we suspected, Longford did not have too much to see, not even the locals seemed too impressed with what the place had to offer (or at least our B&B host, which strongly recommended us to avoid going to the centre) but they directed us to a little

Marzia Bisognin/Arquivo do fotógrafo

MadPhotosPI/Shutterstock

harbour, which my dad and I enjoyed seeing. It made for the perfect evening, just walking around a cute village, looking at the pretty fields dotted by sheep and cows.

So on our final day, we had to reach Belfast. As we were driving, my dad stated that in this trip we didn't see any castles, other than their ruins, and how we definitely all expected to see more of them popping up. Just as he said that, this castle showed up.

We stopped in front of it, but unfortunately it wasn't open, so we admired it from the outside and then quickly left again.

In Belfast, we stayed in the Titanic Hotel, and since I've always been quite fascinated with the Titanic, checking out the museum was very cool.

We also of course strolled around the centre, although I would have to say that the best bit was this one road with quirky pubs blending together to create a colourful alley.

The next day we had our alarms set at 3 a.m., so we went to sleep quite early, and even though it was a quick trip, I felt like we had the perfect amount of time in each location, and I got to see everything I was curious about (of course we missed a lot of the south, but for the time we had, I'm happy we managed to stop by these places).

If you want to see more, head over to my channel as I'm about to post the vlog!

Available at: <https://marziaslife.com/2018/07/06/hello-ireland/>. Accessed on: Feb. 25, 2019.

3 Read Marzia's post again and choose the best alternative to complete each sentence.

a. Marzia went to Ireland with...

  ◯ her mother and some relatives.   ◯ her mother and father.

b. After crossing Rope Bridge, they found...

  ◯ a village of fishermen.   ◯ some amazing views.

c. Before arriving in Galway, they stopped in...

  ◯ Londonderry and Sligo.   ◯ Cliffs of Moher.

d. After leaving Galway, they stopped in...

  ◯ Longford.   ◯ Belfast.

4 Answer the following questions according to the text.

a. When they arrived in Londonderry, they had a bad surprise. What was it? How did they solve the problem?

_____

_____

b. What was Marzia's opinion about Galway?

_____

_____

c. At the end of her trip, was Marzia happy or disappointed? Which parts of the text confirm your answer?

_____

_____

d. Considering the places Marzia and her parents visited, which ones would you prefer to visit? Why?

_____

Text 2

5 The blog post below is also from Marzia. Take a quick look at the pictures and read the title. Then check what you can infer.

a. ◯ The blog post focuses mainly in another trip with her family.

b. ◯ The blog post is about a very special day with her friends.

c. ◯ The blog post is about her daily routine.

https://marziaslife.com/

25.

October 22nd, 2017

Another year, another birthday party!

Yesterday was my birthday, which happened to fall on a Saturday, giving me the perfect chance to spend the weekend away. I rented an Airbnb, invited some friends, and celebrated my 25th birthday!

Felix and I arrived in that lovely place on Friday night, so we would be there before the guests, to have the time to decorate the place.

I set everything up in the afternoon. People started arriving at 5:00 p.m. and we planned to spend the night in the house all together.

We spent the evening playing board games and watching a horror. Dan and Phil gifted us their board game Truth Bombs, which is incredibly funny!

Felix managed to get me a birthday cake made – it was pretty last minute – and it tasted great. It was massive.

It was so much fun having all these amazing people under the same roof for a night, and the fact that they were willing to come all the way to Rye (1.5/2 hours away) made me feel special and extremely grateful.

It was a wonderful birthday.

Thank you all so much for the birthday wishes!

Di Studio/Shutterstock

Studio Romantic/Shutterstock

Studio Romantic/Shutterstock

Available at: <https://marziaslife.com/2017/10/22/25/>. Accessed on: Feb. 25, 2019.

6 Now, read the whole blog post and write **T** (true), **F** (false) or **NM** (not mentioned).

a. ◯ Felix is Marzia's best friend.

b. ◯ Felix helped Marzia to organize the party.

c. ◯ Marzia and her friends stayed in a small hotel in the city.

d. ◯ Marzia's friends had to drive for a couple of hours to get to the party.

7 The blog posts you have read are personal ones. Based on their structure, check the characteristics of personal blog posts.

a. ◯ It is based on questions and answers.

b. ◯ Usually the content is about personal experiences.

c. ◯ Some pronouns – such as **I**, **we**, **us** and **myself** – are very common.

d. ◯ Pictures can do more than illustrate, they can be part of the text.

e. ◯ Since posts in personal blogs report experiences, most verbs are in the past form.

8
179 Based on what you've read about Marzia's experiences, write a personal blog post to be published in a blog.

a. Choose a topic to write about: an amazing trip; an important school event; a great achievement etc.

b. Consider the blog post characteristics and write a draft of it in your book.

c. Show it to your teacher and classmates and make the necessary corrections.

d. Write a final version and publish it. You can create a vlog and publish it as well.

◀ ▶ | www.hello!teens.com/blog   _ ⊡ ✕

TIPS FOR LIFE

Right to leisure

1 In pairs, read the text and discuss it.

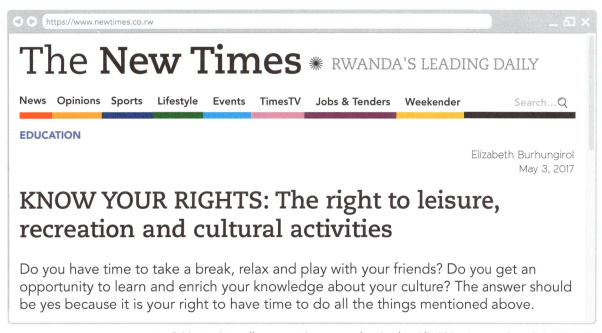

The New Times ✳ RWANDA'S LEADING DAILY

News Opinions Sports Lifestyle Events TimesTV Jobs & Tenders Weekender Search...🔍

EDUCATION

Elizabeth Burhungirol
May 3, 2017

KNOW YOUR RIGHTS: The right to leisure, recreation and cultural activities

Do you have time to take a break, relax and play with your friends? Do you get an opportunity to learn and enrich your knowledge about your culture? The answer should be yes because it is your right to have time to do all the things mentioned above.

Available at: <https://www.newtimes.co.rw/section/read/211693>. Accessed on: Feb. 25, 2019.

2 Still in pairs, create a poster with the theme "Know your rights: leisure, recreation, and culture".

TO LEARN MORE

To know more about the Brazilian Estatuto da Criança e do Adolescente (ECA), go to: <https://www.childfundbrasil.org.br/blog/eca-estatuto-da-crianca-e-adolescente/>. Accessed on: Feb. 26, 2019.

CHECK YOUR PROGRESS	😃	😐	☹️
Idioms and leisure activities			
Simple Past – regular verbs			
Listening			
Speaking			
Reading			
Writing			

1 Find and circle the Simple Past form of the verbs from the box. Then choose three verbs and write sentences using them.

cry	dance	die	drop	look	like
listen	play	start	stay	visit	walk

L	O	O	K	E	D	T	E	L	I	W	E	R	W	W
O	T	U	T	J	G	J	U	Z	U	Z	Z	U	A	U
H	T	P	Q	J	L	I	K	E	D	Q	K	T	L	A
J	S	L	U	S	U	Q	U	H	K	U	K	J	K	Z
S	T	A	R	T	E	D	T	D	H	Z	U	H	E	A
T	A	Y	Y	U	U	L	I	S	T	E	N	E	D	C
Q	Y	E	O	D	R	O	P	P	E	D	T	N	Y	R
Q	E	D	H	I	O	G	V	I	S	I	T	E	D	I
T	D	H	U	E	H	E	J	H	Q	L	Z	M	Y	E
O	Z	H	Q	D	J	D	A	N	C	E	D	K	I	D

a. _____

b. _____

c. _____

2 Read the sentences and underline the correct form of Simple Past or Past Continuous.

a. My father and my mother **was/were walking** in the park last Sunday afternoon.

b. They **didn't visit/visited** the World Exhibition Center yesterday.

c. Leo **play/played** soccer with Allan yesterday morning at school.

d. **Did/Was** you enjoy Thomas' birthday party last week?

e. We were **washed/washing** my uncle's car last Saturday morning when grandma **called/were calling** us.

f. John **played/was playing** chess with his father when his mother **ask/asked** him to take out the garbage.

3 Complete the sentences with **there was** or **there were**.

a. _____ a big tsunami in Japan in 2011.

b. _____ twelve boys playing soccer in the rain last night.

c. _____ a big birthday party going on at Leo's house on the weekend.

d. I was late for dinner yesterday because _____ a big car accident on the road.

e. _____ an awesome sci-fi movie on TV last Sunday.

f. _____ three newborn kittens at the pet shop last Tuesday.

4 Read about Allan's daily routine. Then write a paragraph about what he did yesterday using the Simple Past.

a. Allan stays in bed until 10:00 a.m.

b. He doesn't play soccer in the morning.

c. In the afternoon he studies for his school exams.

d. He dances at Pepper's Dance Club.

e. He doesn't watch TV in the evening.

_____

_____

_____

_____

_____

5 Now, it's your turn! What did you do yesterday? (List at least 5 actions you did to form a paragraph.)

_____

_____

_____

_____

_____

_____

_____

Unit 3 REMARKABLE PEOPLE

Vinnie Zuffante/Michael Ochs Archives/Getty Images

Richard Stonehouse/Getty Images

RALPH GATTI/Agence France-Presse

dpa picture alliance/Alamy/Fotoarena

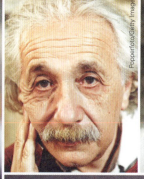

Popperfoto/Getty Images

Flip Schulke/Corbis/Getty Images

Wendy Stone/Corbis/Getty Images

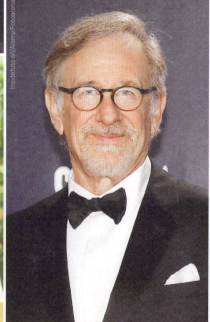

Insidefoto srl/Alamy/Fotoarena

Samir Hussein/WireImage/Getty Images

Lisa O'Connor/ZUMA Wire/Alamy/Fotoarena

ES Imagcry/Alamy/Fotoarena

1 Look at the pictures and talk to your classmates.

   a. Do you know any of these people? What did they do to become remarkable?

   b. What qualities do you think they have?

2 Read and listen to the dialog. Then act out.

15 **Carol:** Hey boys, did you do your homework?

Allan: Yes, we did. We were doing research of a remarkable person when we found an interesting guy called Mohamad.

Carol: Where is he from? And what did he do that is so special?

Bart: He is from Syria. He built a school for refugee children when he was only 12 years old.

Allan: During the research, we found out that, nowadays, there are 200 children attending his school and they learn English, Math and Photography.

Bart: Also, he won the International Children's Peace Prize in 2017.

Carol: Really? What a coincidence! I researched a young woman called Malala and she also won the same prize in 2014!

Bart: How nice! Isn't she from Pakistan?

Carol: Yes, her father was a teacher and he always encouraged her to go to school and learn. She became an activist for the women's rights and girl's education in Pakistan.

Allan: We definitely found two remarkable people!

Carol: Sure we did!

3 Read the sentences and check the correct one.

   a. ◯ Mohamad is from Pakistan.

   b. ◯ Mohamad built a school for refugee children.

   c. ◯ Only Malala won an International Peace Prize.

TO LEARN MORE

Read about the International Children's Peace Prize at: <https://kidsrights.org/childrenspeaceprize>. Accessed on: Feb. 21, 2019.

1 Look at the map and answer the questions about Mohamad.

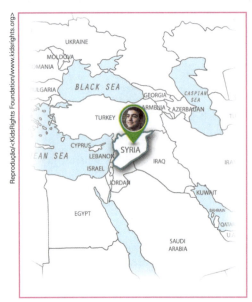

Available at: <https://kidsrights.org/mohamad-al-jounde>. Accessed on: May 20, 2019.

a. What prize did he win in 2017?

_____

b. What is his nationality?

_____

c. What do you know about his country?

_____

TO LEARN MORE

To read Mohamad's life story go to: <https://kidsrights.org/mohamad-al-jounde>. Accessed on: Feb. 12, 2019.

2 Now read a short biography about Mohamad Al Jounde. Then mark **T** (true) or **F** (false) and correct the false ones.

https://kidsrights.org/

Mohamad's story

Mohamad, 16 years old, grew up in Syria, but fled for Lebanon when life became too dangerous at home. Like thousands of other refugee children in the country, he couldn't go to school, so he set out to make a difference for children in the same situation. Together with his family, Mohamad built a school in a refugee camp where 200 children now access their right to education. At the age of 12, he was already teaching Math and photography. He helps children to heal, learn and have fun with games and photography. Mohamad is a natural storyteller, raising awareness about the challenges facing refugee children by bringing their stories to a wider audience.

Available at: <https://kidsrights.org/mohamad-al-jounde>. Accessed on: Feb. 21, 2019.

a. ◯ As a refugee he couldn't go to school.

b. ◯ He built a school in Syria.

c. ◯ He was 10 years old when he built a school.

d. ◯ The children play games and learn photography at Mohamad's school.

3 What is your opinion about Mohamad's work? What message does he want to give to the world? Discuss with a classmate.

A WORD WORK

1
16 What do these remarkable people do? Complete the sentences with words from the box. Then listen and check.

> filmmaker   singer   pediatrician   activist   businessman
> painter   author   physicist   actress

a.

Bill Gates is an American

_____,
magnate, author,
philanthropist, and
humanitarian.

b.

J. K. Rowling is a British

_____, best known
for writing the *Harry Potter*
series. She was praised for
making reading "cool" as
she received an important
award during a ceremony
at Edinburgh University.

c.

Zilda Arns was a Brazilian

_____ and
aid worker. She became
internationally known by
her humanitarian work that
included the poor and the
elderly.

d.

Wangari Maathai was a
Kenyan environmental

political _____. She
became the first African
woman to receive the
Nobel Peace Prize, in 2004.

e.

Steven Spielberg is an

American _____.
He is considered one of
the most popular directors
and producers in film
history.

f.

Picasso was a Spanish
talented artist:

_____, sculptor,
ceramicist, poet and
playwright. He was the
co-founder of Cubism.

g.

John Lennon was the

legendary _____, songwriter and peace activist who co-founded The Beatles. He was British.

h.

Emma Watson is an

_____, model, and activist. She was born in Paris and performed in all eight *Harry Potter's* movies.

i.

Albert Einstein was a German-born theoretical

_____

who developed the Theory of Relativity.

LANGUAGE TIPS

> **Actress:** a woman who performs in plays and movies, especially as her job. Many women performers prefer to be called actors instead of actresses.
> Available at: <www.macmillandictionary.com/dictionary/british/actress>. Accessed on: March 3, 2019.

2 Find and circle the following professions in the wordsearch.

filmmaker	singer	pediatrician	activist	businessman
painter	author	physicist	actress	

```
B  U  H  V  D  O  A  W  T  P  F  G
U  E  P  P  H  Y  S  I  C  I  S  T
S  A  I  E  E  S  I  L  L  E  O  E
I  E  I  T  D  E  I  M  S  S  A  T
N  D  N  E  E  J  M  T  I  I  C  S
E  E  T  D  N  A  O  T  N  N  T  S
S  O  E  E  K  Y  L  D  G  G  I  H
S  I  R  E  O  M  C  N  Y  E  V  L
M  P  R  A  U  T  H  O  R  R  I  T
A  L  G  R  A  C  T  R  E  S  S  A
N  R  G  Y  S  E  A  P  E  D  T  F
P  E  D  I  A  T  R  I  C  I  A  N
```

3 Which other remarkable people would you add to the list?

_____

4 What career would you like to pursue? Talk to a classmate and explain the reasons for your choice.

TIME FOR A GAME

Let's play **Stop** and **Scrambled Words**!

1 Read the following sentences from the dialog on page 45 and underline the correct option.

> **Carol:** Hey boys, **did** you **do** your homework?
>
> **Allan:** Yes, we **did**. […] we **found** an interesting guy called Mohamad. [...]
>
> **Bart:** He is from Syria. He **built** a school for refugee children when he **was** only 12 years old.

a. The verbs in bold are in the **present/future/past** tense.

b. "Did" is the auxiliary verb used in the **past/present/future** tense with **regular verbs/ irregular verbs/both regular and irregular verbs**.

c. The words "found" and "built" are **regular/irregular/infinitive** verb forms of the verbs "find" and "build" in the **future/past/present** tense.

2 Go back to the dialog on page 45 and find two other examples of irregular verbs and two examples of regular verbs in the past.

Regular verbs in the past	Irregular verbs in the past

3 Read and complete the chart.

Simple Past – Irregular verbs					
Affirmative form		**Interrogative form**		**Negative form**	
I		I		I	
You		you		You	**didn't** (did + not)
He	**found** something interesting.	he	_____ anything interesting?	He	
She		she		She	
It		_____ it		It	_____ anything interesting so far.
We		we		We	
You		you		You	
They		they		They	

GRAMMAR HELPER

Go to page 170.

4 Read Malala's biography and complete it with the verbs from the box. Follow the example.

~~spoke out~~   became   gave   began   wrote   returned
took   won   closed   shot   moved

www.hello!teens.com/biography

Malala Yousafzai

Malala Yousafzai (born July 12, 1997, Mingora, Swat valley, Pakistan) is a Pakistani activist who __spoke out__ against the Taliban's prohibition on the education of girls.

On September 1, 2008, her father, a social activist and educator, _____ Malala to a local press club to protest against the school closings, and she

_____ her first speech – "How Dare the Taliban Take Away My Basic Right to Education?".

On January 15, 2009, Taliban _____ the schools for girls and Malala _____ writing regularly for BBC about her daily life. She _____ from January through the beginning of March of that year.

On October 9, 2012, a Taliban gunman _____ Malala in the head while she was coming back home from school. Malala _____ with her family to Birmingham (UK), where she recovered and _____ to her studies and to activism.

In 2014 she _____ the youngest person to win the Liberty Medal, awarded to public figures who fight for people's freedom throughout the world. In the same year, she _____ the Nobel Prize, becoming the youngest Nobel laureate.

She currently studies Philosophy, Politics and Economics at the University of Oxford in the United Kingdom.

Based on: <www.britannica.com/biography/Malala-Yousafzai>. Accessed on: Feb. 12, 2019.

5 Create five questions about Malala using the words given. Make the necessary changes to the verbs. Then answer the questions and compare them in pairs.

a. where/Malala's father/take/her/on September 1, 2008?

_____

b. how old/be/Malala/when/she/give/her first speech?

_____

c. when/Taliban/close/the schools for girls?

_____

d. when/Malala/write/for BBC?

_____

6 Read the following sentence paying attention to the highlighted words. Check the correct statements about them.

> [...] We **were searching** for a remarkable person when we **found** an interesting guy called Mohamad.

a. ◯ In this sentence, an action was in progress in the past when another one happened at a specific time.

b. ◯ Both actions were happening at the same time in the past.

c. ◯ The action described by the verb in the Simple Past (**found**) interrupted the action described in the Past Continuous (**were searching**).

GRAMMAR HELPER

Go to page 171.

7 Go back to the text in activity 4 and underline one example of the Past Continuous and Simple Past being used in the same sentence.

8 Read and complete the chart.

Past Continuous & Simple Past	
Past Continuous & Simple Past: **when, while**	Malala was going home **when** it happened.
	It happened **while** Malala was going home.
	We found Mohamad Al Jounde's biography _____ we were searching on the Internet.
	We were searching on the Internet _____ we found Mohamad Al Jounde's biography.

9 Make sentences with the words given, adjusting the verbs accordingly.

a. I/go to school/yesterday morning/my friend/remind/me/about our homework.

_____

_____

b. My English teacher/talk about remarkable people/the principal/come in.

_____

_____

c. We/discuss our research about remarkable people/a friend/suggest Wangari Maathai.

_____

_____

◀10 Read these quotes paying special attention to the words in blue.

> "**Some** painters transform the sun into a yellow spot, others transform a yellow spot into the sun." – Pablo Picasso
>
> Available at: <www.brainyquote.com/quotes/pablo_picasso_100865>. Accessed on: Feb. 20, 2019.

> "I went from being totally unknown and never acting professionally to being in a major movie and being very famous. It all happened so quickly, I didn't have **any** time to work things out. It's been pretty scary at times." – Emma Watson
>
> Available at: <www.brainyquote.com/quotes/emma_watson_574379>. Accessed on: Feb. 20, 2019.

◀11 Now underline the correct word to complete the sentences appropriately.

a. We use *some* and *any* to describe **quantities/qualities**.

b. **Some/Any** is more commonly used in affirmative sentences.

c. **Some/Any** is more commonly used in negative and interrogative sentences.

◀12 Complete the sentences in the chart according to the previous activity.

Some & Any	
Affirmative	I have _____ useful books to do our research.
Interrogative	Do you have _____ ideas about the homework?
Negative	Sorry, I don't have _____ ideas at the moment.

LANGUAGE TIPS

> **Some** can also be used in interrogative sentences when we are offering something and we expect an affirmative answer. For example:
> *Would you like some juice?*
> **Any** can also be used in affirmative sentences meaning "qualquer/quaisquer". For example:
> *You can choose any book.*

◀13 Complete the following quotes with **some** or **any**.

a. "Courage is the most important of all the virtues because without courage you

can't practice _____ other virtue consistently." — Maya Angelou (poet, storyteller, activist)

Available at: <www.brainyquote.com/quotes/maya_angelou_120859>. Accessed on: Feb. 20, 2019.

b. "Do the right thing. It will gratify _____ people and astonish the rest."
— Mark Twain (writer)

Available at: <www.brainyquote.com/quotes/mark_twain_122044>. Accessed on: Feb. 20, 2019.

LISTEN AND SPEAK

1 You are going to listen to a story called "I will be a hummingbird", told by Wangari Maathai. Read the following words from the story and answer: what do you think the story is about? Talk to a classmate.

discourage   forest   stream   animals   fire   drop   overwhelmed   water   best

2 Listen to the story and check your predictions from activity 1.
17

3 In pairs, read these sentences that summarize the story and match them to the images.

a. All the animals in the forest feel very powerless except this little hummingbird.

b. A forest is consumed by a fire.

c. The hummingbird wants to do something about the fire. It takes a drop of water and puts it on the fire.

d. The hummingbird turns to the other animals and tells them, "I am doing the best I can."

e. The other animals say to the hummingbird, "What do you think you can do? You are too little. This fire is too big."

1.

2.

3.

4.

5.

4 Listen to the story again and put the images in order according to what you hear.
18

The correct order is: _____

5 Read Wangari Maathai's advice. Do you agree with it?

> "We should always be like a hummingbird. I may feel insignificant, but I certainly don't want to be like the animals watching the planet goes down the drain. I will be a hummingbird, I will do the best I can."
>
> Available at: <http://www.youtube.com/watch?v=IGMW6YWjMxw>. Accessed on: Feb. 9, 2019.

6 In pairs, think about a problem and a simple action you can take to help solve it. Follow the instructions below.

a. Think about a problem. These images might give you some ideas.

Plastic pollution

Abandoned animals

Students without school supplies

b. Think about something you can do to improve these situations. For example: recycle; donate school materials and clothes; organize a campaign etc.

c. Talk to a classmate about it. Here you find some useful expressions:

- To improve the situation of… I can…

- I/We can… to help…

- I can't solve the problem of… by my own, but I can…

PRONUNCIATION CORNER

1 Listen to the tongue twisters and act out.

19

1. Susan and Steve treat sick people at the Southern Hospital.

Susan and Steve save sick people at the Southern Hospital.

Save our Souls Susan and Steve!

2. When a doctor doctors a doctor, does the doctor doing the doctoring doctor?

And the doctor wants to be doctored?

3. The firefighter fights against fire.

4. The teacher is teaching the students.

2 Let's practice some tongue twisters.

20
- Susan and Steve save sick people at the Southern hospital.
- When a doctor doctors a doctor, does the doctor doing the doctoring doctor?

READ AND WRITE

1 The following text is about Nelson Mandela. What do you know about him? Share it with your classmates.

2 The text about Nelson Mandela is a biography. What kind of information do you expect to find in it?

3 Read the whole biography and answer the questions that follow.

www.hello!teens.com/biography

Nelson Mandela

Rolihlahla Mandela was born into the Madiba clan in the village of Mvezo, South Africa, on July 18, 1918 and died on December 5, 2013 in Johannesburg, South Africa. He got the nickname Nelson from a teacher in school when he was seven years old.

Mandela was a civil rights activist, a lawyer and the president of South Africa from May 10, 1994 to June 14, 1999.

He fought against Apartheid, a system where non-white citizens were segregated and did not have the same rights as white citizens. Mandela dreamed of a democratic and free society where people had equal rights and opportunities.

Mandela got his law degree at University of Witwatersrand, where he met some activists that were also against Apartheid.

Nelson Mandela became a leader in the African National Congress (ANC). In 1962, he was arrested because he led the anti-Apartheid movement and was accused of conspiring to overthrow the State. The South African government accused him of terrorism and sent him to prison for 27 years.

Mandela was awarded the Nobel Peace Prize in 1993 because he ended the Apartheid system. He continued his efforts to end Apartheid until all citizens of all races were allowed to vote in the 1994 election.

Mandela Day is held annually on July 18. In this day, people devote 67 minutes to help others, one minute is counted for every year Mandela served his country.

mark reinstein/Shutterstock

a. What was the Apartheid system?

_____

_____

_____

b. What is the origin of the nickname "Nelson"?

_____

_____

_____

c. Why was he sent to prison?

_____

_____

_____

4 Copy the parts of the biography that confirm the statements below.

a. Mandela's effort to end segregation was successful.

_____

_____

_____

_____

_____

b. Every year, on July 18, South Africans honor Mandela and show gratitude to their leader.

_____

_____

_____

_____

_____

5 What do you think about Mandela's legacy to South African people?

TO LEARN MORE

To know more about Nelson Mandela's life and achievements, watch the movie *Invictus* (2009). Check out the trailer available at: <https://www.imdb.com/title/tt1057500/>. Accessed on: May 7, 2019.

Text 2

6 Do you like quizzes? Where do you usually find them? Talk to your classmates.

7 Without consulting the biography, answer this quiz about Mandela. Then swap quizzes with a classmate and correct his/her answers. What were your scores?

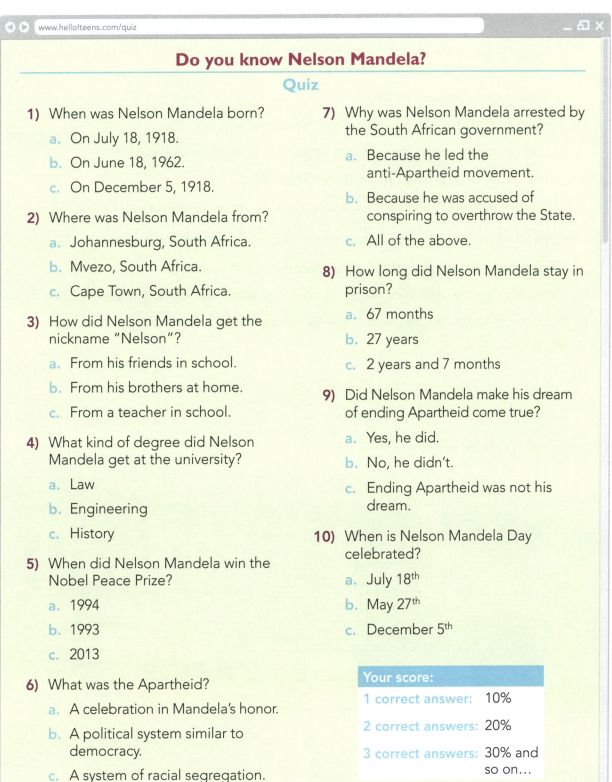

www.hello!teens.com/quiz

Do you know Nelson Mandela?

Quiz

1) When was Nelson Mandela born?
   a. On July 18, 1918.
   b. On June 18, 1962.
   c. On December 5, 1918.

2) Where was Nelson Mandela from?
   a. Johannesburg, South Africa.
   b. Mvezo, South Africa.
   c. Cape Town, South Africa.

3) How did Nelson Mandela get the nickname "Nelson"?
   a. From his friends in school.
   b. From his brothers at home.
   c. From a teacher in school.

4) What kind of degree did Nelson Mandela get at the university?
   a. Law
   b. Engineering
   c. History

5) When did Nelson Mandela win the Nobel Peace Prize?
   a. 1994
   b. 1993
   c. 2013

6) What was the Apartheid?
   a. A celebration in Mandela's honor.
   b. A political system similar to democracy.
   c. A system of racial segregation.

7) Why was Nelson Mandela arrested by the South African government?
   a. Because he led the anti-Apartheid movement.
   b. Because he was accused of conspiring to overthrow the State.
   c. All of the above.

8) How long did Nelson Mandela stay in prison?
   a. 67 months
   b. 27 years
   c. 2 years and 7 months

9) Did Nelson Mandela make his dream of ending Apartheid come true?
   a. Yes, he did.
   b. No, he didn't.
   c. Ending Apartheid was not his dream.

10) When is Nelson Mandela Day celebrated?
   a. July 18th
   b. May 27th
   c. December 5th

Your score:
1 correct answer: 10%
2 correct answers: 20%
3 correct answers: 30% and so on…

8 Check the alternatives that complete the sentence: some questions in the quiz present...

a. ◯ a piece of advice.

b. ◯ date of his death.

c. ◯ historical context of Mandela's life.

d. ◯ some accomplishments throughout his life.

9 All the sentences below are characteristics of the text genre quiz. Underline the ones you can recognize in the quiz about Mandela.

a. Usually quizzes present a title.

b. You can find quizzes on newspapers, magazines, and websites.

c. Questions are objective and can be organized in multiple-choice.

d. Some quizzes can present more than 10 questions.

e. There is a score at the end, so you can check out your performance.

10 Now it's up to you. In small groups, create a quiz. Follow the steps below.

181

a. Choose an interesting theme and do some research about it.

b. Write 10 objective and clear multiple-choice questions about the theme chosen.

c. Show them to the teacher and make all the necessary adjustments.

d. Keep an answer key.

_____
_____
_____
_____
_____
_____
_____
_____
_____
_____
_____
_____

11 Follow your teacher's instructions to take part in a contest of quizzes.

TIPS FOR LIFE

Women empowerment

1 Read the quotes and check the correct sentences.

Joseph Sohm /Shutterstock

1 "Every person who has ever achieved anything has been knocked down many times. But all of them picked themselves up and kept going, and that is what I have always tried to do."

Available at: <www.nationalgeographic.com/environment/great-energy-challenge/ 2011/wangari-muta-maathai-a-life-of-firsts/>. Accessed on: Feb. 28, 2019.

2 "African women in general need to know that it's ok for them to be the way they are – to see the way they are as a strength, and to be liberated from fear and from silence."

Available at: <www.greenbeltmovement.org/node/515>. Accessed on: Feb. 28, 2019.

Wangari Maathai, Kenyan environmentalist and political activist.

○ In quotes 1 and 2, the main idea is "strength".

○ In quote 1, the message is "we can fall, get up and continue our journey".

○ In quote 2, the message is that African women should be aware of their strength.

○ In quote 2, the main idea is the empowerment of women all over the world.

2 Think about a remarkable Brazilian woman. Why is she remarkable? Do you admire her?

TO LEARN MORE

Wangari Maathai (1949-2011) founded the Green Belt Movement in the 1970s seeking to promote environmental conservation in Kenya and Africa. To know more about her, go to <https://nobelwomensinitiative.org/laureate/wangari-maathai/>. Accessed on: Feb. 20, 2019.

CHECK YOUR PROGRESS	😃	😐	🙁
Professions			
Simple Past (irregular verbs)			
Simple Past & Past Continuous			
Listening			
Speaking			
Reading			
Writing			

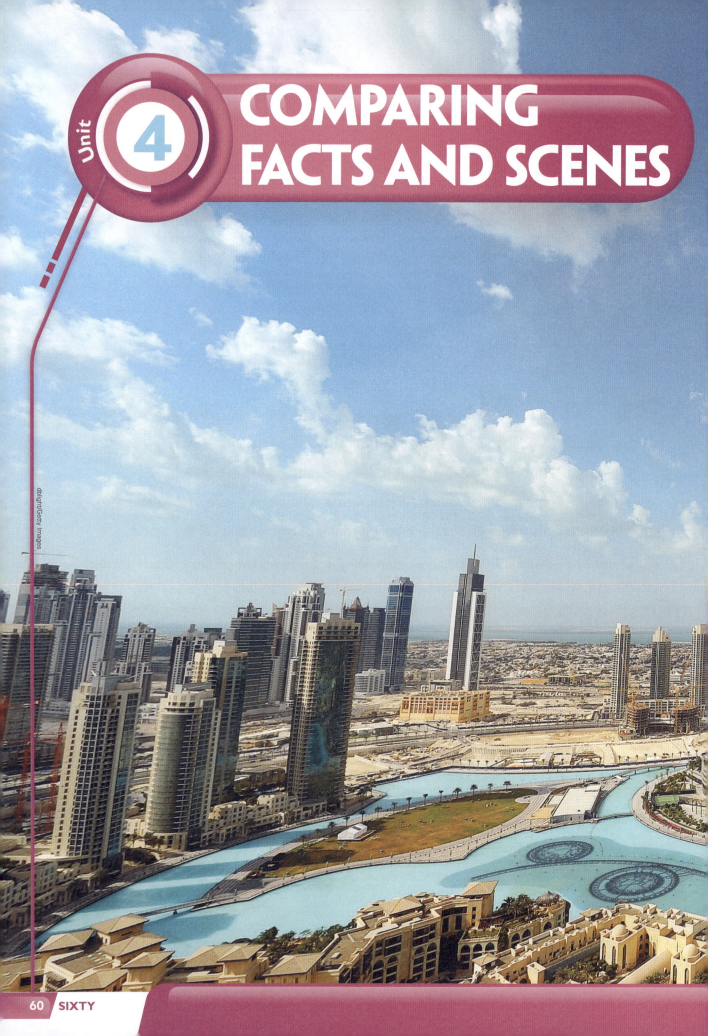

dbiight/Getty Images

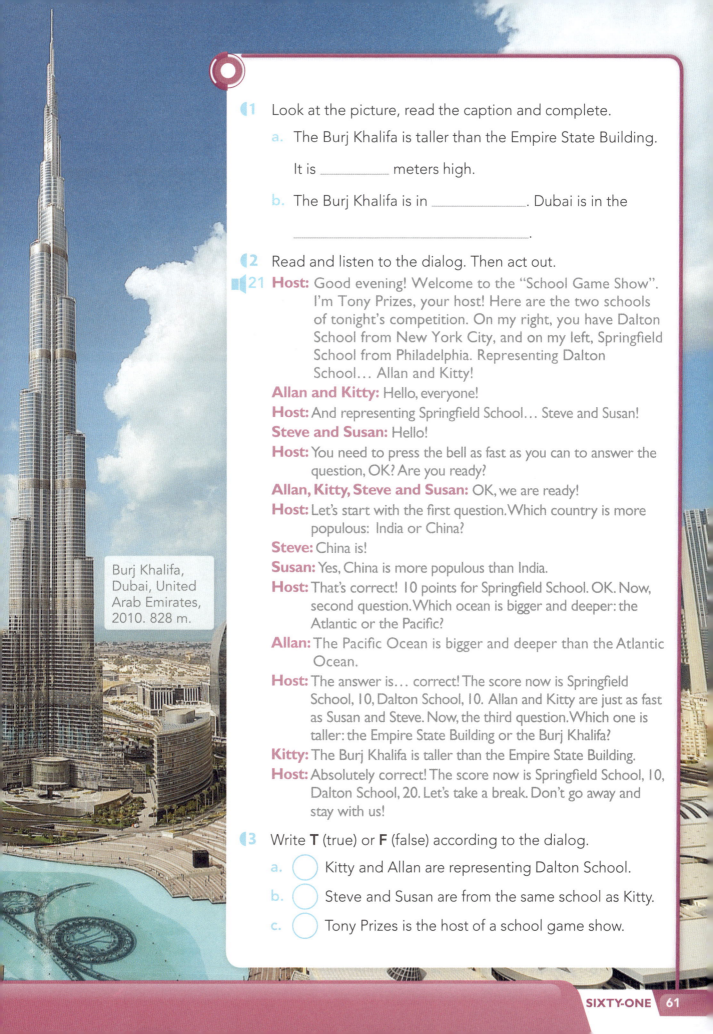

Burj Khalifa, Dubai, United Arab Emirates, 2010. 828 m.

1 Look at the picture, read the caption and complete.

a. The Burj Khalifa is taller than the Empire State Building.

It is _____ meters high.

b. The Burj Khalifa is in _____. Dubai is in the

_____.

2 Read and listen to the dialog. Then act out.

21

Host: Good evening! Welcome to the "School Game Show". I'm Tony Prizes, your host! Here are the two schools of tonight's competition. On my right, you have Dalton School from New York City, and on my left, Springfield School from Philadelphia. Representing Dalton School… Allan and Kitty!

Allan and Kitty: Hello, everyone!

Host: And representing Springfield School… Steve and Susan!

Steve and Susan: Hello!

Host: You need to press the bell as fast as you can to answer the question, OK? Are you ready?

Allan, Kitty, Steve and Susan: OK, we are ready!

Host: Let's start with the first question. Which country is more populous: India or China?

Steve: China is!

Susan: Yes, China is more populous than India.

Host: That's correct! 10 points for Springfield School. OK. Now, second question. Which ocean is bigger and deeper: the Atlantic or the Pacific?

Allan: The Pacific Ocean is bigger and deeper than the Atlantic Ocean.

Host: The answer is… correct! The score now is Springfield School, 10, Dalton School, 10. Allan and Kitty are just as fast as Susan and Steve. Now, the third question. Which one is taller: the Empire State Building or the Burj Khalifa?

Kitty: The Burj Khalifa is taller than the Empire State Building.

Host: Absolutely correct! The score now is Springfield School, 10, Dalton School, 20. Let's take a break. Don't go away and stay with us!

3 Write **T** (true) or **F** (false) according to the dialog.

a. ◯ Kitty and Allan are representing Dalton School.

b. ◯ Steve and Susan are from the same school as Kitty.

c. ◯ Tony Prizes is the host of a school game show.

1 Read the texts and complete the chart. Then answer **T** (true) or **F** (false).

India is also known as the Republic of India. It is a big country located in South Asia, being the seventh largest country by area in the world. Having more than 1.3 billion people, it is also the second most populous country and the most populous democracy around the globe.

China, whose official name is the People's Republic of China (PRC), is a country located in East Asia. It's the world's most populous country, holding a population of around 1.4 billion people. Having an area of approximately 9,600,000 square kilometers, it is the third – or fourth – largest country in the world.

	INDIA	CHINA
Area	3,300,000 sq km	
Location	Southern Asia	Eastern Asia
Capital	New Delhi	Beijing
Population		
Population growth rate	1,17%	0,41%
Population below poverty line	21,9%	3,3%
Life expectancy	68,8 years	75,7 years

Based on: ‹www.indexmundi.com/factbook/compare/india.china›. Accessed on: Feb. 26, 2019.

a. ◯ China is more populous than India.

b. ◯ India is larger than China.

c. ◯ India is poorer than China.

d. ◯ People in China live longer than people in India.

e. ◯ Life expectancy in India is higher than in China.

2 Which country would you like to visit: China or India? Why?

WORD WORK

1 Read and listen to the adjectives. Do these words and their meaning help you describe
🔊 22 people and things? How?

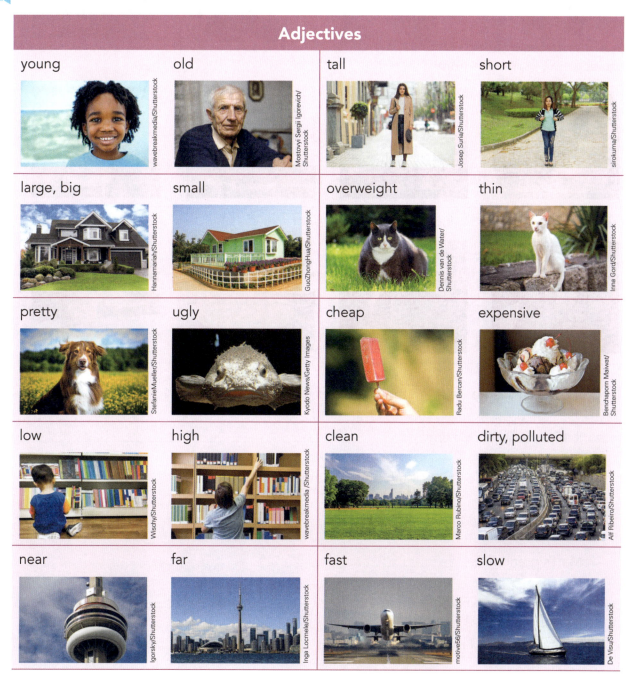

Adjectives

young | **old** | **tall** | **short**

large, big | **small** | **overweight** | **thin**

pretty | **ugly** | **cheap** | **expensive**

low | **high** | **clean** | **dirty, polluted**

near | **far** | **fast** | **slow**

 LANGUAGE TIPS

The adjective **beautiful** is largely used to refer to women while **handsome** is used to refer to men and women.

happy | sad | interesting | boring
quiet | noisy | old | new
simple, easy | difficult, hard | hot | cold

2 Complete the sentences with the adjectives mentioned in activity 1.

a. I think reality shows are _____.

b. Many students don't like Math because they think it is _____.

c. A Ferrari is a very _____ car.

d. Matt's grandpa is _____.

e. Tietê river in São Paulo is _____.

f. The street where I live is _____.

g. My best friend is _____.

TIME FOR A GAME

Let's play **Mime, Where are you?** and **What's missing?**.

FOCUS ON LANGUAGE

1 Look at the image and read its caption. Then complete the chart with the missing information.

Adjective Order

- Adjectives usually go before a noun:

  This is a <u>modern</u> building in Abu Dhabi.

- Adjectives expressing **opinions** (e.g.: good, bad, beautiful, ugly) go before adjectives describing **facts** (e.g.: old, new, big, small):

  This is a **beautiful circular** building in Abu Dhabi.

- When there are <u>two or more adjectives</u>, we use the following order:

A **modern circular** building in Abu Dhabi, United Arab Emirates.

	Opinion	Size	Age	Shape	Color	Origin	Material	Noun
It's a/an	_____	_____	modern	_____	_____	Emirati	glass	building.

2 Unscramble the sentences. Pay attention to the adjective order.

a. attraction/in/Sugarloaf Mountain/touristic/Rio de Janeiro/main/is/the/.

_____

b. deep/and/north/Amazonas/Brazil/of/large/a/is/river/in/the/.

_____

c. great/ancient/pyramids/Egypt/in/the/did/see/you/?

_____

d. this/local/a/building/architect/designed/huge/beautiful/modern/.

_____

3 Choose one building in your city and, in your notebook, write a sentence describing it. Use some adjectives in the appropriate order. Then share it with a classmate.

GRAMMAR HELPER

Go to page 171.

4 Read the following sentences from the dialog on page 61. Then answer **T** (true) or **F** (false).

> China is **more populous than** India.
> The Pacific Ocean is **bigger** and **deeper than** the Atlantic Ocean.

These sentences are…

a. ◯ comparing facts and characteristics of places.

b. ◯ describing different qualities of two different environments.

c. ◯ describing two different actions.

d. ◯ indicating that something is superior or inferior than something else in some aspect.

e. ◯ comparing two environments that have equal characteristics.

GRAMMAR HELPER

Go to page 172.

5 In pairs, read the chart and complete it with the missing information. Write examples.

	Comparatives		
Short adjectives	Most adjectives with one syllable: add _____ + _____		
	old cold	old**er than** cold**er** _____	Roma is **older than** São Paulo. _____
	One syllable ending in **-e**: add _____ + _____		
	rare nice	_____ _____	Some animals are **rarer than** others.
	One syllable ending in **one vowel** + **one consonant**: double consonant + add **-er** + _____		
	big hot	big**g**er **than** hot**t**er **than**	Belo Horizonte is **bigger than** Ouro Preto. _____
	Two syllables ending in **-y**: change **-y** into **-i** and add **-er** + _____		
	easy happy	eas**i**er **than** happ**i**er **than**	I think Geography is **easier than** Math. _____
Long adjectives	More than two syllables: **more** + adjective + **than**		
	polluted beautiful	**more** polluted **than** _____	Big cities are **more polluted than** small towns. _____
Irregular comparison	Irregular comparative forms		
	good bad far	**better** **worse** **farther/further**	Some cities are **better than** others are. The book I read last week is **worse than** this one. My grandparents live **farther than** my uncle.

6 Do you know the characters in the picture? Complete the sentences about them using the comparative form of the adjectives given.

a. Fred is _____ than Shaggy. (brave)

b. Shaggy is _____ Fred. (funny)

c. Velma is _____ at solving mysteries _____ Daphne. (good)

d. Daphne is _____ Velma. (elegant)

e. Scooby-Doo is _____ Shaggy. (smart)

© Joe Ruby/Hanna-Barbera

7 Read the sentence from the dialog on page 61 and the comic strip below paying attention to the highlighted words. Then complete the chart.

Allan and Kitty are just **as fast as** Susan and Steve.

© 1990 Bill Watterson/Dist. By Atlantic Syndication/Dist. by Andrews McMeel Syndication

Degrees of Comparison	
Equality (as + adj. + as)	Rome is **as beautiful** _____ Venice.
Superiority (more + long adj. + than)	Tokyo is _____ Lisbon. (modern)
(short adj. + -r/-er + than)	Yes, but Lisbon is _____ Tokyo. (small)
Inferiority (less + adj. + than)	Curitiba is _____ **populous than** New York.
	And New York is _____ **quiet than** Curitiba.
(not so/as + adj. + as)	Yes, and Curitiba is **not so/as crowded as** New York.

8 The students are making comparisons. Let's help them. Complete the sentences using the hints in parentheses.

a. Teacher, this test isn't easy. It's _____ the last one. (equality/difficult)

b. What a horrible sofa! It's _____ these old chairs. (inferiority/comfortable)

c. Look at that boy! He is _____ his father! (equality/tall)

d. Let's buy this cell phone. It's _____ that smartphone. (inferiority/expensive)

9 Let's compare. Look at the pictures and read the information about speed and life expectancy of some amazing animals. Check the wrong sentences according to the charts.

COULANGES/Shutterstock   Umomos/Shutterstock   YukioShimura/Shutterstock

Animal	Life expectancy (years)	Animal	Speed (km/h)
Turtle	100	Cheetah	110
Alligator	50	Lion	80
African elephant	35	Zebra	64
Lion	15	Rabbit	56
Domestic cat	12	Domestic cat	48
Domestic dog	12	Squirrel	19
Giraffe	10	Chicken	14
Mouse	3	Snail	0.4

The World Almanac for Kids. New Jersey, World Almanac Books, 2014.

a. ◯ A domestic dog has a longer life expectancy than a mouse.

b. ◯ A lion is faster than a cheetah.

c. ◯ A domestic cat has the same life span (period of life) of a domestic dog.

d. ◯ A domestic cat isn't as fast as a lion.

e. ◯ A zebra is slower than a rabbit.

LISTEN AND SPEAK

1
23 You are going to listen to part of a radio program describing some animals. Look at the pictures and, in pairs, guess which animals are going to be mentioned. Then, listen and check if you guessed correctly.

a. Raccoons

e. Crowes

b. Elephants

f. Chimpanzees

c. Orangutans

g. Dolphins

d. Pigs

2
24 Listen to the first part of the audio and check the most appropriate option.

a. The program is about…

◯ big animals. ◯ smart animals. ◯ small animals.

b. They are going to present…

◯ five animals. ◯ three animals. ◯ eight animals.

3
25 Listen again and number the pictures of the animals according to their rank in the list.

◀4 Test your memory! In your notebook, create five questions about the animals from this unit and ask a classmate. Then answer his/her questions too.

For example, you can ask questions about…
- the speed of one or two animals.
- their life expectancy.
- their abilities.
- some of their characteristics, making comparisons between them.

PRONUNCIATION CORNER

◀1 Listen to the jazz chant. Then act it out.

🔊26

Higher or lower
Hotter or colder
Taller or shorter
Fatter or thinner

Noisier or quieter
Prettier or uglier
Happier or sadder
Easier or harder

Faster or slower
Cleaner or dirtier
Nearer or farther
Older or younger

Today and forever
Ever and ever
Diversity ever
Bullying never, never!

Nik Neves/Arquivo da editora

◀2 Listen and practice.

🔊27

Higher or lower
Hotter or colder
Taller or shorter
Fatter or thinner
Noisier or quieter
Prettier or uglier
Happier or sadder
Easier or harder

◀3 Now, list some more words with this sound.

READ AND WRITE

Text 1

1 Read the title of the news report and look at the picture attentively. In your opinion, does the picture contribute to make the title more meaningful? Why (not)?

a. ◯ No, it only contributes to brighten the page.

b. ◯ Yes, the picture represents how huge and full of life China is.

2 Read the news report and answer the following question.

www.cbc.ca/news/world/china-population-rises-15-23-million-in-2018-but-rate-slows-1.4986218

China Population Rises 15.23 Million in 2018, But Rate Slows
Government estimates China's population will peak at 1.442 billion in 2029.

China's population rose by 15.23 million people in 2018, marking a continued decrease in the growth rate of the world's most populous nation.

Numbers released by the National Bureau of Statistics on Monday put the population at 1.395 billion in 2018, marking a growth rate of .381 per cent over the previous year.

The total included 30 million more men than women, considered a long-time outcome of the recently abandoned one-child policy under which boys were favoured over girls for cultural reasons.

The government estimates China's population will peak at 1.442 billion in 2029 before beginning to decline the year after.

India, the world's second most populous nation, has also been experiencing slower population growth. Its total population stood at 1.362 billion this month based on United Nations estimates.

China added more than 17 million people to its population in 2016 and 2017 following the scrapping of the one-child policy, but the effect hasn't endured.

Care for the elderly is a rising government concern as the working-age population continues to fall as a percentage of the total.

Chinese increasingly enjoy better living standards, education and health care, but a yawning gap between the wealthy and poor has experts saying the country will grow old before it grows rich. […]

Traffic on the Nanpu Bridge in front of the Shanghai skyline last year. The country's population is still growing, but at a slower rate.

Johannes EISELE/Agência France-Presse

Available at: ‹www.cbc.ca/news/world/china-population-rises-15-23-million-in-2018-but-rate-slows-1.4986218›. Accessed on: Feb. 17, 2019.

What is the reason mentioned for the population decline?

○ It's a consequence of the one-child policy.

○ Because many Chinese families are poor and avoid having kids.

○ Economic growth in China has declined.

3 Read the statements and answer **T** (true) or **F** (false). Copy the parts of the news report that support your choices.

a. ○ Before 2018, population growth rate of China was not declining.

_____

_____

b. ○ There are more men in China than women.

_____

_____

c. ○ India is considered the most populous nation in the world according to the United Nations.

_____

_____

d. ○ The majority of population in China is rich.

_____

_____

4 What do the numbers below refer to? Match the columns.

a. 15.23 million: ○ added population in 2016 and 2017.

b. 1.442 billion: ○ China's estimated population for 2029.

c. 17 million: ○ Chinese population that rose by 2018.

5 The news report is full of numbers. Check the resources that you believe could help readers to understand all those numbers.

○ graphs   ○ pie charts   ○ fractions

○ charts   ○ percentages

Text 2

6 Read the title of the following article and make some predictions. What are the possible economic implications of India's population growth?

a. Food shortage

b. Poor health services

c. Rise of unemployment rates

Read the article in full. Then match the questions to the answers.

India's Population Will Soon Be Bigger Than China's. And The Economic Implications Are Huge.

Adam Shirley

By 2022, India's population will have overtaken China's to become the largest in the world, according to a United Nations report.

As the world's two most populous nations, China and India already have well over 1 billion people each. But while China's population is forecast to level out in the 2020s at around 1.4 billion, India's population is expected to carry on soaring.

Here's what these seismic demographic changes will mean for both countries – and the world.

[...]

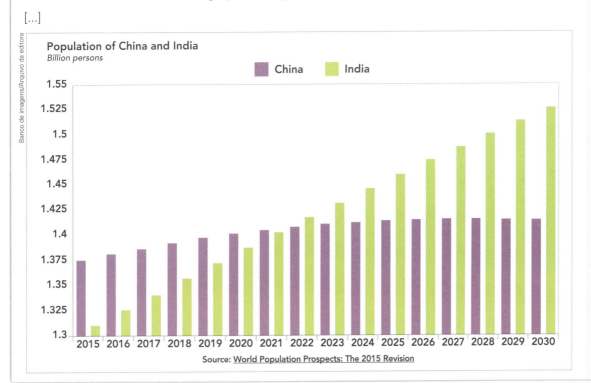

Population of China and India
Billion persons

Source: World Population Prospects: The 2015 Revision

Available at: <www.weforum.org/agenda/2016/06/when-will-india-have-more-people-than-china/>. Accessed on: Feb. 26, 2019.

a. According to the article, what are the most populous countries in the world?

b. What does the United Nations report claim about India?

c. According to what you have read, which country will face more harmful effects of overpopulation in the future?

◯ India.

◯ China and India.

◯ India will become the most populous country in the world.

8 Look carefully at the graph. Then answer the questions.

a. What do the colors purple and green represent in the graph?

_____

_____

b. What do the numbers in the horizontal line represent?

_____

_____

c. What about the vertical line?

_____

_____

d. Do you think graphs can help you to understand articles? How?

_____

_____

9 In pairs, prepare an oral presentation to your classmates. Use graphs to illustrate the topic.
183 Follow the steps below.

• Choose an interesting topic and do some research about it.

• Gather all the information and produce a draft of a graph.

• Write a text to introduce your oral presentation.

• Show the graph and the text to your teacher.

• Do the necessary adjustments and write a final version of the text.

• Produce the final version of the graph in a paperboard.

• Pin the graph on the wall or on the board so everyone can see it.

• Present your work.

TIPS FOR LIFE

Thinking of cultural diversity

◀1 Look at the picture and answer: What do you understand by cultural diversity?

Rawpixel.com/Shutterstock

To learn more about cultural diversity, watch the video "Cultural differences – from all over the world… to Italy". Available at: <www.youtube.com/watch?v=vO6N0ha22Mk>. Accessed on: Mar. 6, 2019.

◀2 Diversity comes from the comparison between people, places, cultural traits, and other social features. In pairs, read the definition of **cultural diversity** and compare it with your answer in activity 1.

Noun

1. the cultural variety and cultural differences that exist in the world, a society, or an institution.

Available at: <www.dictionary.com/browse/cultural-diversity>. Accessed on: Mar. 6, 2019.

◀3 In groups of four discuss the questions below.

a. What traditions are commonly shared with your family and community?

b. Compare Brazilian traditions (people, food, music, celebrations, movies, hobbies) to the traditions of a country in Asia (like China, India or other).

c. Make a list of five comparisons and share it with your classmates.

CHECK YOUR PROGRESS	😃	😐	🙁
Adjectives			
Comparisons			
Degrees of comparisons			
Listening			
Speaking			
Reading			
Writing			

1 Complete the sentences with **some**, **any**, **many** or **much**.

a. Would you like to drink _____ coffee?
No, thank you.

b. How _____ sugar do we have in the cupboard?

I'm not sure. I think we have _____.

c. There isn't _____ food in the fridge. Is there _____ bread left?

Yes, there is _____ on the table. Just bring home _____ milk.

d. How _____ apples are there in the basket, Susan?
There are a dozen apples, mom.

2 Form sentences with the words given and use the verbs accordingly.

a. My father/help me/with my research/his boss/call/him.

_____

b. I/do/English homework/brother/study/History.

_____

c. The History teacher/teach some/important facts about Brazil/the English teacher/talk about important people around the world.

_____

_____

3 Read the sentences and check the correct order of adjectives to complete the gaps.

a. My daughter Liz has _____ hair.
   ◯ a beautiful long black   ◯ a long black beautiful

b. It was such _____ day so John and I decided to go to the beach.
   ◯ a sunny lovely   ◯ a lovely sunny

c. My mother bought _____ kitchen table.
   ◯ an old, wooden   ◯ a wooden, old

d. Jessica lives in ————————— apartment.

○ a lovely modern ○ a modern lovely

e. Austin drives ————————— sports car.

○ a fast, Italian, shiny red ○ a shiny red, fast, Italian

4 Write three questions about Malala Yousafzai using the words given and the correct verb tenses. Then answer the questions based on the text from page 50.

a. what/prizes/Malala/win/in 2014/?

_____

_____

b. what/she/study/now/?

_____

_____

c. where/she/study/?

_____

_____

5 Write questions (Q) with the comparison **as... as**. Then complete the answers (A) appropriately.

a. rabbits/fast/turtles

Q: _____

A: No, rabbits are _____ (superiority) turtles.

b. Paul/friendly/Mary

Q: _____

A: No, Paul is _____ (inferiority) Mary.

c. Mr. Green/short/Mr. Brown

Q: _____

A: Yes, Mr. Green is _____ (equality) Mr. Brown.

d. apples/expensive/pears

Q: _____

A: No, apples are _____ (inferiority) pears.

e. Alaska/cold/Toronto

Q: _____

A: No, Alaska is _____ (superiority) Toronto.

THE AMAZING HUMAN BODY

Nathan King/Alamy/Fotoarena

1 Look at the picture and discuss with your classmates.

   a. What is this picture related to?

   b. Which words come to your mind when you see it?

   c. Do you know any uncommon facts about the human body? Which ones?

2 Read and listen to the dialog. Then act out.

28 **Leo:** We have to talk about our Science fair project. Whose book is this?

Allan: It's mine. We can use it to do our research. What body part or organ are we going to choose?

Jim: Let's see... What about doing a project about the brain?

Leo: That's a great idea! First, we have to divide our tasks. Who is going to do research on the Internet?

Jim: I can do that!

Leo: I have a nice poster which shows every part of the brain.

Allan: Great! We can make a model of it!

Jim: What does your Science book say about the brain, Allan?

Allan: The brain is an interesting and complex organ in the human body that looks like a cauliflower and consists of over ten billion nerve cells. It has two distinct halves.

Leo: And it also creates the most interesting thoughts, the most exciting dreams, the best and the worst emotions.

Jim: Cool! Let's start our brain project!

Allan: But first, let's grab a bite to eat to keep our brains functioning well.

3 Read the dialog again and check the true sentences.

   a. ◯ The boys have a Science fair project to do.

   b. ◯ The brain is responsible for creating thoughts, dreams and emotions.

   c. ◯ Leo is going to search for some information on the Internet.

   d. ◯ The brain is a complex organ in the human body.

1 Did you know that the human brain is one of the most powerful organs in the body? Check it out!

https://kids.nationalgeographic.com

Your amazing brain

You carry around a three-pound mass of wrinkly material in your head that controls every single thing you will ever do. From enabling you to think, learn, create, and feel emotions to controlling every blink, breath, and heartbeat — this fantastic control center is your brain. It is a structure so amazing that a famous scientist once called it "the most complex thing we have yet discovered in our universe."

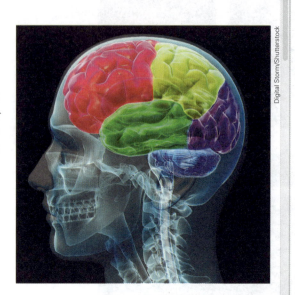

Your brain is faster and more powerful than a supercomputer.

[...] No computer can come close to your brain's awesome ability to download, process, and react to the flood of information coming from your eyes, ears, and other sensory organs.

Exercise helps make you smarter.

It is well known that any exercise that makes your heart beat faster, like running or playing basketball, is great for your body and can even help improve your mood. But scientists have recently learned that for a period of time after you've exercised, your body produces a chemical that makes your brain more receptive to learning. [...]

Available at: <https://kids.nationalgeographic.com/explore/science/your-amazing-brain/#brain.jpg>.
Accessed on: Feb. 27, 2019.

2 Answer **T** (true) or **F** (false) according to the text. Correct the false statements.

a. ◯ Our brain can be compared to a supercomputer.

_____

b. ◯ Exercising is only good to make us fit.

_____

c. ◯ Our heart is responsible for controlling our emotions.

_____

d. ◯ The brain is considered the most complex organ in the human body.

_____

3 In pairs, find and underline comparative sentences in the text. Then talk about them.

WORD WORK

1   Let's learn the name of some parts of the human body. Listen and repeat.

29

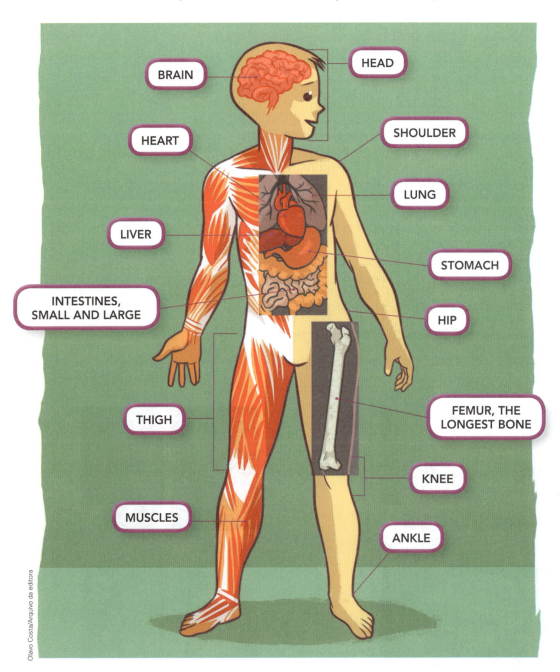

BRAIN

HEAD

HEART

SHOULDER

LUNG

LIVER

STOMACH

INTESTINES, SMALL AND LARGE

HIP

THIGH

FEMUR, THE LONGEST BONE

KNEE

MUSCLES

ANKLE

Olavo Costa/Arquivo da editora

TO LEARN MORE

From the skin that covers us to the heart that pumps our blood, the human body is a complex machine whose parts must work together to keep us healthy and alive. For more information about the human body, go to: <www.sciencekids.co.nz>. Accessed on: Feb. 14, 2019.

2 Read the definitions and write in the boxes the name of the missing parts.

a. In the ⬚⬚⬚⬚⬚ , oxygen from the air you breathe is passed into the blood.

b. It mixes the food and changes it into assimilable substances:

⬚⬚⬚⬚⬚⬚⬚

c. It pumps blood around the body carrying oxygen to every cell:

⬚⬚⬚⬚⬚

d. It produces bile, which helps us digest food:

⬚⬚⬚⬚⬚

e. The human skeletal system is made of ⬚⬚⬚⬚⬚ that hold our body upright.

3 Read the questions and match them to the picture that represents the correct answer.

a. What is the most important organ of our body?

b. What is the human body's biggest organ?

c. What is the smallest part of the human body?

d. What is the longest bone in an adult human body?

Geinz Angelina/Shutterstock

the skin

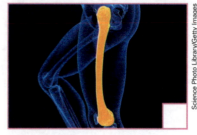
Science Photo Library/Getty Images

the femur

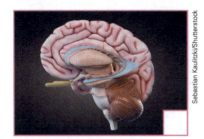
Sebastian Kaulitzki/Shutterstock

the brain

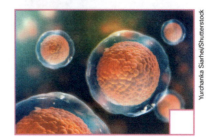
Yurchanka Siarhei/Shutterstock

the cell

TIME FOR A GAME

Let's play **Bingo** and **Brainstorm**!

1 Read the sentence from the dialog on page 79 and the image beside it. Then complete the sentences that follow with the words from the box.

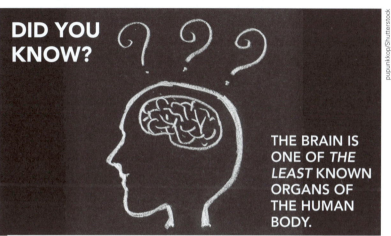

Leo: And it also creates **the most interesting** thoughts, **the most exciting** dreams, **the best** and **the worst** emotions.

DID YOU KNOW?

THE BRAIN IS ONE OF *THE LEAST* KNOWN ORGANS OF THE HUMAN BODY.

| long   opposite   superior   worst (2×)   short   the   best (2×)   inferior   least |

a. The sentences indicate that one thing is extremely _____ or

_____ to others of the same type or group.

b. The word **most** is usually placed before _____ adjectives to talk about something or someone that has more of a particular quality. When the adjective is

_____, we usually add **-st** or **-est** to it.

c. The word _____ is used to talk about something or someone that has less of a quality.

d. The article _____ is usually used with superlative adjectives.

e. Some adjectives have irregular forms, for example: _____ is the superlative

form of good and _____ is the superlative form of bad.

f. The sentence "the best and the worst emotions" express _____ ideas.

The _____ means of excellent type or quality while the _____ means of low excellence or quality.

GRAMMAR HELPER

Go to page 173.

2 Help your teacher to elaborate a chart about the superlative form. Then complete it.

3 Read the following curiosities and complete them with the adjectives from the box. Use the superlative form.

sensitive(2x)   hard   large   powerful   common   fast   long

a. The femur is _____ bone in the human body.

b. Some of _____ growing bones in the human body are the leg bones. They grow quickly.

c. The skin is _____ organ in the human body. It covers all your body.

d. One of _____ areas in the human body are the hands. In contrast,

_____ area is the middle of the back.

e. The brain is _____ organ in your body. It controls everything.

f. In Brazil, _____ blood types are O and A. Almost 90% of the population has these blood types.

4 Look at the pictures and write sentences with the comparative and superlative forms of the given adjectives.

a.

John/tall/Paul: _____

John/tall/in my class: _____

b.

Lilly/thin/Petunia: _____

Lilly/thin/at home: _____

c.

Patricia/happy/Cynthia: _____
Patricia/happy/on the school team:

_____

5 Complete the sentences using the comparative or superlative form.

a. The… book I know is…

_____

b. My friend is very honest, but…

_____

c. Your T-shirt is too large…

_____

d. My best friend is one of the…

_____

e. The… video game I know is…

_____

f. My cousin's bike is good, but…

_____

6 In pairs, read the dialog then ask and answer questions using the comparative or superlative form.

Some adjectives you can use:		Some topics you can talk about:	
Fast	Small	Animals	TV series, movies
Dangerous	New	The human body	School subjects
Bad	Good	People	Cities, countries etc.
Happy	Difficult	Games	

7 Read the comic strip paying attention to the highlighted word and complete the chart.

Relative pronouns		
_____	things, people and animals	The Science book _____ was used for the project is very interesting. The boy _____ is talking to Hobbes is Calvin.
which	things and animals	The Science fair in _____ I participated was a huge success. Hobbes looks very happy, _____ is a good thing.
_____	people and sometimes pet animals	Calvin, _____ is staring at Hobbes, thinks it's difficult to argue with happy people.
whose	people and animals (possessive meaning)	Calvin has a friend _____ dream is to be in a big sunny field.

8 Complete the sentences using **that**, **which**, **who**, or **whose**. Then compare your answers in pairs.

GRAMMAR HELPER

Go to page 174.

a. The students _____ are doing a project about the brain need to do some online research.

b. All the systems in our body are like members of a team _____ job is to keep you alive and healthy.

c. There are important points _____ the students need to consider in their project about the brain.

d. The heart is one of our vital organs, _____ means it keeps us alive.

◀1 Listen to a teacher talk about the human brain. Look at the picture and read the sentences from activity 2. What words and expressions from activity 2 do you think will be mentioned? Circle them.

◀2 Listen to a teacher talking about the human brain and check the information you heard.

🔊30

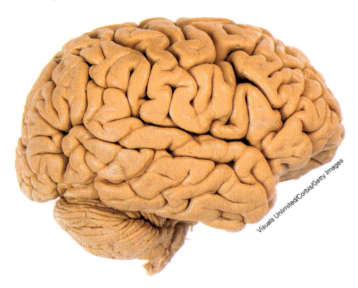

Visuals Unlimited/Corbis/Getty Images

a. ◯ The cerebrum is smaller than the cerebellum.
   ◯ The cerebellum is smaller than the cerebrum.
   ◯ The cerebrum and the cerebellum are the same size.

b. ◯ Because of the brain, you can stand up straight.
   ◯ Because of the cerebrum, you can stand up straight.
   ◯ Because of the cerebellum, you can stand up straight.

c. ◯ The two parts of your brain control the left side of your body.
   ◯ The left side of your brain controls the right side of your body.
   ◯ The right side of your brain controls the right side of your body.

d. ◯ The cerebrum controls the voluntary muscles of your body.
   ◯ The cerebellum controls the voluntary muscles of your body.
   ◯ The cerebrum controls balanced movement and coordination.

e. ◯ To give your brain a workout, you can play music.
   ◯ To give your brain a workout, you can go to sleep.
   ◯ It is not possible to give your brain a workout.

3 Listen one more time and write what can be done to exercise and protect our brains.

🔊 31

_____

_____

_____

4 You are going to make a presentation about an organ of the human body. In groups of four students, do some research, organize your ideas and present them.

PRONUNCIATION CORNER

1 Listen and act out the jazz chant.

🔊 32

Nik Neves/Arquivo da editora

The **poor**est or the **rich**est
The **tall**est or the **short**est
The **fast**est or the **slow**est
The **heavi**est or the **light**est

The best or the worst
The **young**est or the **old**est
The **big**gest or the **small**est
The **hap**piest or the **sad**dest

The most ex**pen**sive
The most **in**teresting
The most **dan**gerous
The most, the most...

It doesn't **mat**ter
They can be **bet**ter
They are part of a game
They won't stay the same
They get a**wards** and re**wards**
They are **Gui**ness' **rec**ords!

2 Listen and practice. Then choose three of the superlatives below and make a sentence.

🔊 33

The poorest
The richest
The tallest
The shortest

The fastest
The slowest
The (more/less) expensive
The (more/less) interesting

_____

_____

READ AND WRITE

Text 1

1 Quickly read the text below. What is it about?

2 Read and take the quiz.

www.allthetests.com

Do You Know How to Take Care of Yourself?

You are the most important person in your life, find out if you know how to take care of yourself.

1. Do you exercise regularly?

a. Not really, but I try to walk everywhere I go.

b. I have a sports practice a few times a week.

c. I take a dance lesson once a week.

d. Yes, I work out at the gym everyday.

2. Do you take time for yourself and to relax?

a. No, I'm too busy.

b. Every chance I get, I read or watch a movie.

c. Every day I take time for myself to do something relaxing like yoga.

d. I go for a massage once in a while.

3. What do you eat?

a. I'm a picky eater but try to stay away from junk food.

b. Anything fast and simple.

c. Lots of fruits, veggies and whole grains.

d. A bit of everything from the 4 groups.

4. Do you eat breakfast?

a. Yes, I eat something like cereal or a toast.

b. I drink coffee or juice.

c. Yes, I eat a full breakfast with eggs, toast, fruits.

d. No, I'm never hungry in the morning.

5. What does your night routine looks like?

a. I remove my makeup and brush my teeth.

b. I shower, moisturize, remove my makeup and brush my teeth.

c. I go straight to bed.

d. I brush my teeth.

6. How many hours of sleep do you get every night?

a. 6 to 7.

b. 8 or more.

c. Less than 4.

d. 4 to 5.

7. Do you drink a lot of water?

a. No, water doesn't taste like anything.

b. Yes, but I should drink more.

c. Yes, but I also drink juice and/or milk.

d. Yes, at least 8 glasses a day.

8. How many times a day do you brush your teeth?

a. In the morning and at night.

b. In the morning.

c. After every meal.

d. I forget so I chew gum.

Available at: <www.allthetests.com/quiz30/quiz/1345038625/Do-you-know-how-to-take-care-of-yourself>. Accessed on: Feb. 27, 2019.

3 Check out your score: do you know how to take care of yourself?

Question	Points	Score
1	a. 2 b. 1 c. 3 d. 0	
2	a. 3 b. 0 c. 1 d. 2	
3	a. 3 b. 1 c. 0 d. 2	
4	a. 2 b. 1 c. 3 d. 0	
5	a. 0 b. 3 c. 2 d. 1	
6	a. 1 b. 0 c. 3 d. 2	
7	a. 3 b. 1 c. 0 d. 2	
8	a. 2 b. 3 c. 1 d. 0	
	Total:	

(24-18 pts)   You take very good care of yourself! You have a good hygiene and healthy habits. You are on the right track!

(17-12 pts)   You know what it takes to take care of yourself but don't always take the time. Don't forget that you are the most important person in your life. Pamper yourself!

(11-0 pts)   You take little time to take care of yourself. Always remember that you are important and worth the time for a healthy and balanced life. Exercise, good hygiene and a healthy diet are a good start!

4 Do you agree with the result? Do you think you can promote changes in your life to make it better?

_____

_____

_____

5 Read the sentences below and check what you can infer from the quiz.

a. ( ) Eating habits are crucial when it comes to being in good health.

b. ( ) Keeping physically active is as important as having good hygiene and good eating habits.

c. ( ) Leisure time is irrelevant when it comes to having a healthy life.

d. ( ) Anyone who cares about health could be interested in this quiz.

e. ( ) Drinking lots of water may help you prevent diseases.

f. ( ) Good hygiene is not important for staying healthy.

6 Are there other aspects you consider important when talking about healthy lifestyles? Talk to your classmates.

Text 2

7 Read the title and the navigation menu below. What kind of information do you expect to find in the text?

_____

8 Read the fact list and check **yes** or **no**.

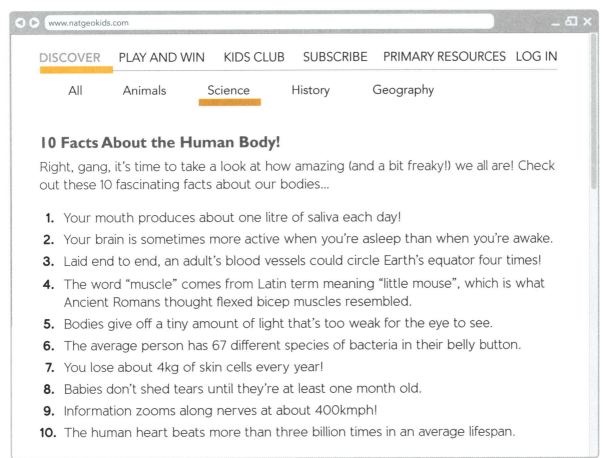

Available at: <https://www.natgeokids.com/nz/discover/science/general-science/15-facts-about-the-human-body/>.
Accessed on: Feb. 27, 2019.

	Yes	No
There are long paragraphs in the text.		
The list is numbered.		
There are concise sentences.		
The items are related to the same topic.		

9 Read the sentences and write **T** (true) or **F** (false) according to the text.

a. ◯ Adult's blood vessels are longer than the Earth's equator.

b. ◯ The brain is used more when we are awake than when we are asleep.

c. ◯ "Little mouse" refers to the word "muscle".

d. ◯ Our body loses 4kg of skin cells a week.

10 In your opinion, which item from the text is the most interesting? Which one is the scariest? Why? Talk to your classmates about it.

11 In pairs, choose one interesting or curious topic: it can be related to science, nature, history, animals or geography. Write a fact list about it. Follow the steps below.

    a. Choose an interesting topic and do some research about it.

    b. Gather all the information and organize a list.

    c. Make sure all the items in the list are about the same topic and the information is clear and concise.

    d. Choose the appropriate tone for your text. Consider your target audience.

    e. Write a draft and show it to the teacher.

    f. Do all the necessary adjustments and write the final draft in your book.

    g. Add some pictures or drawings for your list to be more attractive.

12 Follow your teacher's instructions to create a mural of interesting facts.

185

TIPS FOR LIFE

Good health habits

1 Look at the picture: What is it about? Write a caption for it.

_____

_____

_____

_____

2 Interview a classmate and discover what she/he does to stay healthy.
Do you...?

a. ◯ have a lot of vitamins

b. ◯ stay active daily

c. ◯ eat high fiber food regularly

d. ◯ take a shower every day

e. ◯ brush your teeth after meals

f. ◯ drink a lot of water

g. ◯ exercise and practice sports

h. ◯ wash your hands before meals

i. ◯ eat fruit and vegetables

j. ◯ eat any junk food

3 In groups, compare your answers. Are they similar or different? Then write three other things people can do to stay healthy.

_____

_____

CHECK YOUR PROGRESS	😃	😐	🙁
The human body			
Adjectives – Superlative form			
Relative pronouns			
Listening			
Speaking			
Reading			
Writing			

DIGITAL WORLD

Tonis/Shutterstock

1 Look at the picture and discuss with your classmates: What does "digital world" mean?

2 Read and listen to the dialog. Then act out.

34 **Carol:** I am going to play a new game tonight.

Kitty: Really? What game is it?

Carol: It's an online game called MegaCity.

Jim: It sounds interesting. What is it about?

Carol: It's a building game where you create a well-functioning city.

Jim: Is it an interactive game?

Carol: Yes, you can exchange materials with other players in order to build what you want.

Kitty: Isn't this kind of game dangerous?

Jim: What do you mean, Kitty?

Kitty: I mean giving personal information to anonymous strangers.

Jim: I see! My mom always talks to me about it. She says never to give any information online, like name, address, age, passwords.

Carol: Your mom is right, Jim. My uncle says the same. He understands nothing about technology, but he knows a lot about online security!

Kitty: We teach the adults about technology and they teach us about security. This way everybody can have fun in the virtual world!

Carol: It's exactly what I am going to do tonight… Have some fun!

3 Write **T** (true) or **F** (false) according to the dialog.

a. ◯ Carol is going to play a multiplayer online game tonight.

b. ◯ In MegaCity, players can create a nice city.

c. ◯ For Jim's mom, when online, you can give personal information.

d. ◯ Carol's uncle understands everything about technology.

1 Read the sentence and answer: Do you agree with it? Why (not)? Discuss with your classmates.

> We teach the adults about technology and they teach us about security.

2 Read the cartoons and check the correct items.

A

> HONEY, HOW DO I SEND THIS BABY PICTURE TO YOUR MOM'S CELL PHONE?

> ATTACH THE PHOTO TO EMAIL, ENTER HER NUMBER AND PRESS "SEND".

In this family, the expert in technology is the...
- ◯ baby.
- ◯ father.
- ◯ mother.

For the boy, the one responsible for his life...
- ◯ are the parents.
- ◯ is technology.
- ◯ is only the mother.

B

"No, I didn't download you off the Internet, I gave birth to you. End of discussion!"

3 In pairs, read the cartoons again and answer the questions.

a. What do both cartoons have in common?

_____

b. Which cartoon best represents the sentence from activity 1? Why?

_____

4 How did people use to live without internet? Share your ideas with your classmates.

A WORD WORK

◀1
🔊35
Listen and repeat. Then write in your notebook full sentences about how you use the internet. Read the example.

I play games on the computer.

Post videos and photos

Play games

Download softwares

Read

Enter chat rooms

See photos

Listen to music

Create and post content

Study

◀2 What else can you do on the internet? Talk to a classmate and write some ideas in your notebook.

_____

_____

_____

3 Is internet and IM language the same as every day spoken language? Look at some abbreviations and acronyms. Then complete the IM conversation with the appropriate ones.

Ilustrações: Nik Neves/Arquivo da editora; emojis: tanaya/Shutterstock

LANGUAGE TIPS

The **IM language**, or "instant messaging language", consists of short phrases and abbreviations. It's commonly used on social networks and messenger apps.

IM Dictionary: a shorthand to speed up IM

IC = I see	**R** = are	**!** = I have a comment
BFF = best friend forever	**2NTE** = tonight	**RUT** = are you there?
TY = thank you	**?** = I have a question	**IDK** = I don't know
THX = thanks	**Luv** = love	**GTG** = got to go
SMS = short message service	**2 moro** = tomorrow	**YW** = you're welcome
ASAP = as soon as possible	**U** = you	**BTW** = by the way
CUL = see you later	**BC** = because	**BIF** = before I forget
JK = just kidding	**T@YL** = talk to you later	**Y** = why

TIME FOR A GAME

Let's play **The Alphabet Game** and **Spelling Bee**!

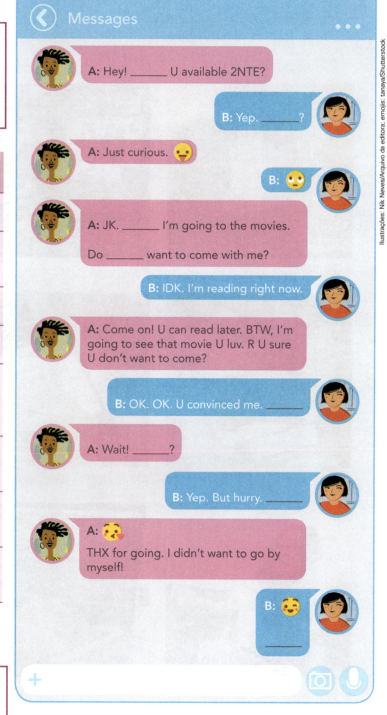

11:37

Messages

A: Hey! _____ U available 2NTE?

B: Yep. _____?

A: Just curious. 😜

B: 🙄

A: JK. _____ I'm going to the movies. Do _____ want to come with me?

B: IDK. I'm reading right now.

A: Come on! U can read later. BTW, I'm going to see that movie U luv. R U sure U don't want to come?

B: OK. OK. U convinced me. _____

A: Wait! _____?

B: Yep. But hurry. _____

A: 😘 THX for going. I didn't want to go by myself!

B: 😊

4 In pairs, do some research and list other abbreviations people usually write when texting in English. Then add to the list the abbreviations and acronyms you use when texting in Portuguese.

_____

_____

FOCUS ON LANGUAGE

1 Read these sentences from the dialog on page 95, paying special attention to the words in bold. Then check the correct option.

> **Carol:** I **am going to play** a new game tonight. [...]
> **Carol:** It's exactly what **I am going to do**.

GRAMMAR HELPER

Go to page 174.

We use **going to** to talk about…

a. ◯ the future, expressing plans and intentions.

b. ◯ something that is happening in the moment of speaking.

c. ◯ an action that was happening in a specific time in the past.

2 Now, read the comic strip below and answer the following questions. Compare your answers in pairs.

a. How does the computer organize photos?

_____

b. Why does the lady think the computer lost its mind?

_____

c. What does the man think the computer can do?

_____

d. In the last scene, the man is…

◯ being sarcastic.   ◯ telling the truth.

3 Read the comic strip again, paying attention to the highlighted words. Then underline the option that completes the sentence correctly.

> We also use "going to" to talk about **predictions/advices** for the future, when we have facts that prove them or we are certain they are going to happen.

4 Read the chart below and complete it with the missing information.

Future – going to		
Affirmative form: subject + verb to be (present) + going to + main verb in the infinitive (without *to*).		
I _____ You _____ She _____ We _____	**going to**	**create** a website using this new software.
Negative form: subject + verb to be (present) + not + going to + main verb in the infinitive (without *to*).		
He _____ You _____ They _____	_____ **to**	**play** online games tomorrow.
It _____	**going to**	**crash**. It's working perfectly.
Interrogative form: verb to be (present) + subject + going to + main verb in the infinitive (without *to*).		
_____ **you** _____ **she** _____ **they**	**going** _____	**post** this photo on social media?
***Wh-* questions**		

- Where is she going to post her comment? She _____ post it on her social media account.

- What are you going to do tonight? I _____ video chat with my family.

- When _____ they _____ create your web page?
  They _____ it tonight.

- Who is going to help you create your web page? My mother _____ help me.

- Why aren't you _____ chat with your friends? Because I don't want to.

5 Read the comic strip and check the correct answers.

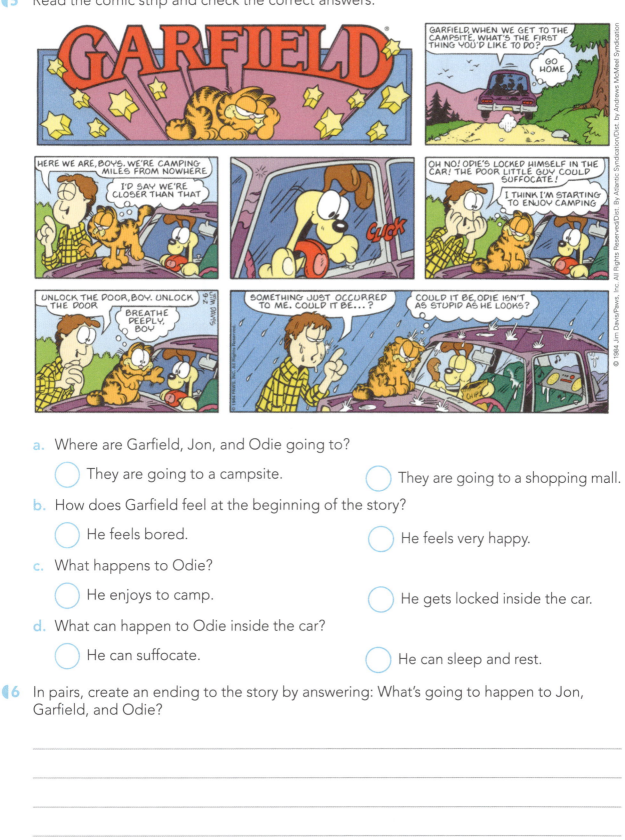

a. Where are Garfield, Jon, and Odie going to?

   ◯ They are going to a campsite.   ◯ They are going to a shopping mall.

b. How does Garfield feel at the beginning of the story?

   ◯ He feels bored.   ◯ He feels very happy.

c. What happens to Odie?

   ◯ He enjoys to camp.   ◯ He gets locked inside the car.

d. What can happen to Odie inside the car?

   ◯ He can suffocate.   ◯ He can sleep and rest.

6 In pairs, create an ending to the story by answering: What's going to happen to Jon, Garfield, and Odie?

_____

_____

_____

_____

_____

7 Read the following extract from an article. Then check the correct options.

◄ ► www.nytimes.com/   _ ⬚ ✕

My selfie, **myself**

Jenna Wortham

"There is a primal human urge to stand outside of **ourselves** and look at **ourselves**," said Clive Thompson, a technology writer [...].

Selfies have become the catchall term for digital self-portraits [...]. Every major social media site is overflowing with millions of them.

Available at: <www.nytimes.com/2013/10/20/sunday-review/my-selfie-myself.html>.
Accessed on: Mar. 5, 2019.

a. According to the article extract, selfies are...

   ◯ digital self-portraits.   ◯ any photos posted on social media.

b. Nowadays, people take selfies because they want to...

   ◯ look at themselves from the outside.   ◯ post millions of portraits online.

8 Read the extract again, paying attention to the pronouns in bold. Then complete the sentences with the words from the box.

> myself   self   selves   ourselves

a. The word _____ refers to *I*.

b. The word _____ refers to *we*.

c. The suffix - _____ is used for singular – *I, you, he, she, it*.

d. The suffix - _____ is used for plural – *we, you, they*.

LANGUAGE TIPS

Selfie is an adaptation of the suffix -*self* that refers to a portrait you take of yourself.

9 Now, complete the sentences with the correct reflexive pronoun.

a. The woman saw _____ in the mirror.

b. When the man is worried, he talks to _____.

c. The new teachers introduced _____ to the students.

d. Be careful, Anna! That iron is very hot. Don't burn _____!

GRAMMAR HELPER

Go to page 175.

◀1 Read the following extract. Then, in pairs, create a short sentence to define cyberbullying.

_____

_____

◀ ▶ | https://www.commonsensemedia.org/ | _ ⊡ ×

What is cyberbullying?

Cyberbullying is the use of digital-communication tools (such as the Internet and cell phones) to make another person feel angry, sad, or scared, usually again and again. [...]

Examples of cyberbullying include sending hurtful texts or instant messages, posting embarrassing photos or video on social media, and spreading mean rumors online or with cell phones.

Available at: <www.commonsensemedia.org/cyberbullying/what-is-cyberbullying>.
Accessed on: Mar. 1, 2019.

◀2
36 You are going to listen to Vanessa's testimonial. Listen to the first part of the audio and check the correct option.

Vanessa describes a cyberbullying situation…

a. ◯ that happened to her.

b. ◯ that happened to a friend.

c. ◯ in which she was involved in as a bully.

◀3
37 Listen to the first part of the audio again and underline the option that best completes each statement. Then check your answers in pairs.

a. When Vanessa first heard about cyberbullying, she though it **could/would never** happen to her.

b. She had a serious fight with her **best friend/boyfriend**.

c. Vanessa's best friend used **social media/e-mail** to write bad things about her.

d. Vanessa **wrote/didn't write** bad things about her best friend.

◀4
38 What do you think Vanessa did about her situation? In pairs, come up with some ideas and take notes in your notebook. Then, listen to the second part of the audio and check your predictions.

Oleg Golovnev/Shutterstock

5 In pairs, listen to the second part of the audio again and answer the questions.

39 a. According to Vanessa, how difficult or easy is it to deal with cyberbullying?

_____

b. Who helped her deal with this situation?

_____

c. What does she recommend for anyone dealing with cyberbullying?

_____

6 You are going to report to your classmates a situation that happened to you. It doesn't need to be about cyberbullying. It can be about anything you would like to share. Follow these steps:

a. Decide what you would like to talk about.

_____

b. Organize what you are going to say and write a draft in your notebook.

_____

c. Give one suggestion for people that go through a similar situation.

_____

_____

PRONUNCIATION CORNER

1 Listen to the jazz chant and act out.

40 **A:** What are you going to do tomorrow?

B: I'm going to play soccer or games.

C: I'm going to create a blog or a photo blog.

D: What are they going to do tomorrow?

A: She is going to play soccer and he's going to create a blog.

D: And you, what are you going to do?

A: I'm going to talk to an old friend from high school.

B and C: An old friend from high school! Awesome!

D: Awesome! Fantastic!

2 Listen and repeat.

41

> cold – gold
>
> class – glass
>
> cat – get
>
> came – game

Text 1

1 In pairs, read the cartoons below and reflect on this question: Are social media friends real friends? Why (not)?

A

"Facebook friends are better than real friends. Nobody on Facebook has bad breath!"

B

"My teacher told me to read for an hour a day. Do Facebook and text messages count?"

C

"When I was a little girl, I had an imaginary friend. Now I have 875 imaginary friends on Facebook."

_____

_____

_____

_____

_____

_____

_____

2 Read the statements below and check the cartoons they refer to.

	Cartoon A	Cartoon B	Cartoon C
a. Social media presents a world where everyone is perfect and has a happy life.			
b. Social media friends are not real.			
c. Spending too much time online can affect school life.			

3 Answer the questions according to the cartoons.

About cartoon A

a. Where are these people?

_____

b. Why is the woman surprised?

_____

c. Do you think the man appreciates his real friends? Why (not)?

_____

About cartoon B

a. Are the characters in the cartoon related?

_____

b. Do you think the woman is sad or angry? Why (not)?

_____

c. What does the boy have in his hands? What does it mean?

_____

About cartoon C

a. In your opinion, why does the woman compare her social media friends to her imaginary friend?

_____

b. Do you think that having 875 social media friends can prevent loneliness? Why (not)?

_____

Text 2

4 Read the text below. What is it about?

a. ◯ It is a poster about cyberbullying.

b. ◯ It is a menu about a new game store.

c. ◯ It is a feature article about a technological event.

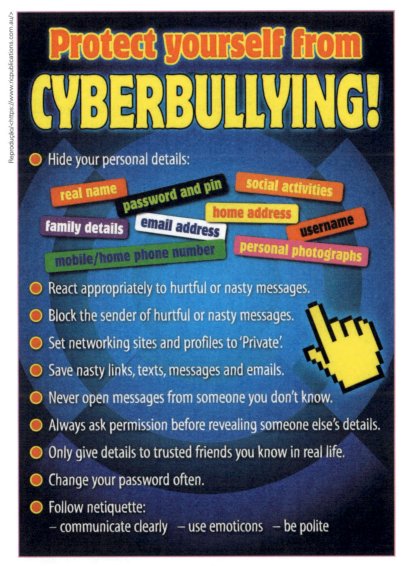

5 Now, read the text and check **T** (true) or **F** (false).

a. ◯ Cyberbullying occurs in digital environments.

b. ◯ You're anonymous online, so you don't need to be polite.

c. ◯ In the digital world, it's important to always change your password.

d. ◯ You can offer some information online, such as your mobile number.

6 What do you do to protect yourself from cyberbullying? Read the text again and circle what you do in a regular basis.

7 Look at the poster on the previous page. Then check the true sentences about this text genre.

a. ◯ The poster is an effective visual communication tool.

b. ◯ The poster presents bright colors to grab readers attention.

c. ◯ The font size of the poster is big, so everyone can easily see it.

d. ◯ The poster has a title, so you can quickly identify its main topic.

e. ◯ The images in the poster support its message and the text is concise.

8 In pairs, design a poster to create awareness about the responsible use of internet. Follow these steps:

187

a. Choose the topic of your poster. Suggestions: netiquette, fake news.

b. Do some research about the chosen topic, taking notes of key information.

c. Write the text for your poster and create a draft of its design.

d. Show the text to your teacher and do all the necessary adjustments.

e. Produce your poster – draw or glue pictures to make it more attractive.

f. Pin your poster at school, so that other students can see and read it.

TIPS FOR LIFE

Online security

1 Answer the questions below.

a. What do you do online?

_____

b. What does "online security" mean to you?

_____

c. In your opinion, are you safe online? Why (not)?

_____

2 Do you worry about safety while surfing the internet? Check the tips you follow.

a. ◯ I always talk to my parents about when and how I use the internet.

b. ◯ I never share personal information, like name, address, and phone number.

c. ◯ I never send photos or say where I am in my free time.

d. ◯ If I receive a message that makes me uncomfortable, I tell my parents or ask an adult for help.

e. ◯ I don't meet in person anyone I have met online, unless an adult accompanies me.

f. ◯ I never share my passwords with anyone except my parents.

3 Now, write a list with tips about safety on the internet.

_____

_____

CHECK YOUR PROGRESS	😃	😐	🙁
Technology and IM language			
Going to – future			
Reflexive pronouns			
Listening			
Speaking			
Reading			
Writing			

1 Complete the sentences with the superlative form of the adjectives.

a. I think Science is _____ (interesting) subject at school.

b. Allan's fourteenth birthday was _____ (happy) day of his life.

c. I ate at _____ (bad) restaurant in town last night.

d. I went to _____ (good) Jota Quest concert yesterday.

e. Paul is _____ (quiet) boy I know.

f. My schoolbag is _____ (big) in the classroom.

2 Check the correct answers to complete the sentences with the comparative form of the adjectives.

a. Brazil is a _____ country, but Canada is _____ Brazil.

  ○ large / larger than   ○ large / large   ○ larger than / large

b. My brother thinks romantic movies are good, but I think sci-fi movies are _____.

  ○ good than   ○ better   ○ more good

c. In Brazil, this year's summer is much _____ last year's.

  ○ the hottest   ○ colder than   ○ hotter than

d. Daniel is _____ his younger brother, Samuel.

  ○ taller than   ○ tall   ○ the tallest

e. Mia is _____ me in Math. She gets higher grades at school all the time.

  ○ smarter   ○ smarter than   ○ the smartest

f. *Han Solo* is _____ movie I have ever seen in my life.

  ○ bad   ○ worse   ○ the worst

3 Read and circle the odd word out.

   a. hand – foot – femur – arm – leg

   b. stomach – finger – intestines – liver – heart

   c. chest – shoulders – eyes – waist – back

   d. ankle – leg – elbow – thigh – knee

4 Match the columns. Pay attention to the relative pronouns.

   a. Matthew knows the family

   b. It is Mike's birthday and he told me

   c. My grandpa has a car

   d. Maria has a daughter

   e. This is a magazine article

   f. Montreal is the beautiful city

   ◯ which is a classic one.

   ◯ whose car we bought.

   ◯ who is coming to his party.

   ◯ which might be interesting to you.

   ◯ where I was born in.

   ◯ whose ambition is to be an actress.

5 Fill in the gaps using the verbs in parentheses in the future with **going to**.

   a. Monica and Charlie _____ (meet) their friends to hang out.

   b. They _____ (walk) to the mall after school this afternoon.

   c. Sandy and Mark _____ (study-negative) in London next semester.

   d. Ellis _____ (come) to the school party with Oliver.

   e. Meredith _____ (take) a selfie with her friends at the park.

6 Write questions according to the answers.

   a. _____

   I'm going to call the doctor at 8:00 a.m. tomorrow.

   b. _____

   Marina is going to buy her grandma a birthday present next Saturday.

   c. _____

   No, we aren't going to buy any fruit in the market.

   d. _____

   My mother is going to bake a chocolate cake tonight.

   e. _____

   Yes, Mike is going to text his friend about the movie.

WARNER BROS./Album/Fotoarena

1 Look at the picture and answer: Do you like science fiction movies? What is the best sci-fi movie in your opinion?

2 Read and listen to the dialog. Then act out.

42 **Carol:** Wow! What a great movie!

Jim: Yeah, it was! I love science fiction movies.

Leo: Me, too. I just wonder… Will the future be better?

Kitty: Yes, I think it will. I imagine everything will be more comfortable and practical.

Carol: And I believe that medicine will be so advanced that people will hardly ever get sick.

Jim: I'm afraid of progress. I think industrial development will harm the environment…

Leo: … and cities will be more populous and polluted.

Carol: I think that this won't happen.

Allan: People will certainly find solutions to new problems.

Leo: OK, guys! Let's finish this conversation someplace else? I am going to the cafeteria. Who wants to join me?

Carol: I'm going with you, Allan! Let's have some orange juice! If I don't drink anything, I will melt.

Everybody: Okey-doke! Great idea!

3 Read the dialog again and check the correct answers.

a. Kitty thinks that the future will be…

◯ more practical.　　　◯ harder.

b. In Allan's opinion, people…

◯ will find solutions to new problems.

◯ won't find solutions to new problems.

c. They are going to continue their conversation…

◯ in the cafeteria.

◯ at Allan's house.

◀1 What will life be like in the future? In pairs, discuss the chart predictions. If you think they will probably happen, write **True**; if you conclude they won't become a reality, write **False**. Add two new predictions to the list.

Year	Predictions	True or False
2040	Electric airplanes will be common.	
2045	Flying cars will be a reality and affordable.	
2050	Bionic parts (human body) will be affordable, existing everywhere.	
2051	There will be a mission to Mars operated by one or more people.	
2054	There will be a lunar base and an observatory on the moon.	
2055	Scientists will discover new earthlike planets.	
2100	Earth population will peak at 20 billion people.	
2150	There will be "a growing of human spare parts" in laboratories.	
2200	Poverty will be eradicated from the world.	
2500	There will be life and communities in other planets.	
3000	We will drive/ride interstellar spacecrafts.	
5000		
7000		
10000	A new *Homo sapiens* will be born!	

Based on: <http://articles.famouswhy.com>; <http://mkaku.org>. Accessed on: Mar. 1, 2019.

1 Look at some movie posters from different film genres. Listen and repeat.

🔊43

Action

Adventure

Animation

Biography

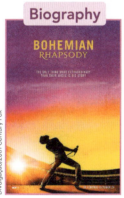

Comedy

Documentary

Drama

Musical

Romance

Science Fiction (Sci-Fi)

Thriller

War

2 Read the film genres from the box and match them to their definitions.

| Fantasy   Mystery   Western |

a. _____: a story or type of literature that describes situations that are very different from real life, usually involving magic.

b. _____: a film based on stories about life in the west of the US in the past.

c. _____: a book, film, or play, especially about a crime or a murder, with a surprise ending that explains all the strange events that have happened.

Available at: <https://dictionary.cambridge.org/pt/>. Accessed on: Mar. 11, 2019.

3 Answer the following questions about your movie preferences.

a. Do you usually go to the movies?

_____

b. How often do you watch movies at home?

_____

c. What is your favorite movie genre?

_____

d. Do you like old movies? Name one.

_____

e. Do you like horror movies? Name one.

_____

f. What is your favorite comedy movie?

_____

g. Do you like and watch Brazilian movies? Why (not)?

_____

_____

h. What is the best Brazilian movie in your opinion? Why?

_____

_____

TIME FOR A GAME

Let's play **Can Game** and **Communicative game**!

FOCUS ON LANGUAGE

1 Read the comic strip and underline the best option to complete each sentence. Then compare your answers with a classmate.

EVANS, Greg. Luan. Dec. 29, 2017. Available at: <www.thecomicstrips.com/store/add.php?iid=166101>. Accessed on: Mar. 15, 2019.

a. It is **Christmas/her dad's birthday**.

b. The girl **gives her dad a present/invites him to help her clean her room**.

c. Her dad is surprised because **she doesn't clean her room very often/he didn't expect any presents**.

d. In the last panel, the words are separated by periods to **give emphasis/express disbelief**.

e. In the last panel, the poster fixed on the wall indicates that the girl is **making a joke/ making a promise**.

2 Read some sentences from the dialog on page 113. Considering them and the comic strip from activity 1, check the appropriate alternatives.

Leo: [...] **Will** the future be better?

Kitty: Yes, I think it **will**.

Jim: [...] industrial development **will** harm the environment [...]

Carol: I think that this **won't** happen.

a. ◯ We use **will** to talk about future actions, predictions, and promises.

b. ◯ **Will** is used to indicate something that happens in the present and continues in the future.

c. ◯ The affirmative form of the future is **will** + *main verb*.

d. ◯ **Won't** is the contraction for the negative form **will** + *not*.

e. ◯ We use **will** when we have evidences about the immediate future.

GRAMMAR HELPER

Go to page 175.

3 Go back to the dialog on page 113 and find other examples of sentences predicting the future.

4 Read the chart and complete it with the missing information. Then write your own examples.

Simple Future (will)			
Affirmative	I/You/He/She/We/They	_____ / 'll	see that action movie tonight. _____
Negative	I/You/He/She/We/They	will + *not* / _____	see that movie tomorrow. _____
Interrogative	_____	I/you/he/she/we/they	see that movie tomorrow? _____

5 Write **will** or **won't** to complete the gaps.

a. _____ your friend come with us to the movies? No, she _____.

b. When _____ you audition for the cast of that superhero movie?

c. Do you think humans _____ live on the Moon in the future? No, I don't.

d. Maybe it _____ be sunny this weekend, maybe it _____!

e. _____ you turn fifteen years old next month? Yes, I _____.

6 Complete the dialogs with the Simple Future verbs from the box.

translate   answer   help   clean

gnepphoto/Shutterstock

a. The camera lenses are so dirty.

_____ them.

b. Can you help me with this German movie synopsis text? I don't understand it.

Sure, _____
it for you.

c. The phone is ringing. The lead actress is calling you.

_____ the phone.

d. The movie set boxes are extremely heavy.

_____ you carry them.

7 Complete the questions with the **Wh- questions** from the box and answer them.

| Who | When | What | Why | Where |

a. _____What_____ will you do today?

   I will prepare for that casting audition.

b. _____ will your father go this afternoon?

   _____

c. _____ will she arrive at home?

   _____

d. _____ will you buy this new camera?

   _____

e. _____ will probably drive you to the movies tomorrow?

   _____

8 Complete the predictions using **will/won't** and the verbs in parentheses.

a. Next year, my baby brother _____ (learn) how to swim.

b. I think I _____ (not play) basketball this month.

c. Next semester, I _____ (study) a lot more for my exams.

d. Probably this year my father _____ (not travel) abroad on business.

9 Write questions for the answers.

a. **Q:** _____

   A: Yes, people will travel in spacecrafts in the future.

b. **Q:** _____

   A: No, industries won't destroy the environment.

c. **Q:** _____

   A: No, I won't watch a war movie. I'll watch some cartoons.

d. **Q:** _____

   A: I'll buy a new computer next weekend.

10 Look at the picture, read the captions and answer the questions. Then, in pairs, compare your answers.

I think the virus will spread all over the world. We have to do something now.

Liam is very emotional. Look at his eyes, he's going to cry.

a. In the first picture, how do you know Liam is going to cry?

_____

b. In the second picture, what is the scientist opinion about the virus?

_____

11 Based on the pictures from activity 10, complete the sentences below with **will** or **going to**.

a. We use _____ to talk about a prediction based on something you can see or hear at the present.

b. We use _____ to talk about a prediction based on an opinion.

12 Look at the pictures and write sentences using **will** or **going to**.

a. it/rain

b. cars/fly

c. she/astronaut

d. he/get a sunburn

_____   _____   _____   _____

_____   _____   _____   _____

LANGUAGE TIPS

Other uses of **will**:
- things you know always happen: This is plastic. It **will** melt if you put it in the oven.
- requests: **Will** you close the door, please?

LISTEN AND SPEAK

1 Look at the movie poster and read the synopsis. Then answer the following questions.

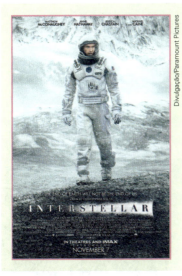

INTERSTELLAR (2014)

Director: Christopher Nolan

Staring: Matthew McConaughey, Anne Hathaway, Michael Caine

Runtime: 2h49min

Plot: In a near future, Earth is devastated by environmental disasters and wars which lead to famine and almost the extinction of the human race. The only way to ensure humans' survival is to find a new home. A team of astronauts travels outside the solar system in the hope to find a planet that has the suitable environment to sustain human life.

a. What is the genre of this movie? _____

b. What happened to planet Earth? _____

c. What solution did the astronauts have? _____

d. Did you see this movie? If so, what do you know about it? Did you like it? If you didn't,

would you like to see it or not? Why? _____

2 You are going to listen to a review of **Interstellar** by a vlogger. Read the pieces of information below and number them according to the order you think they are going to be mentioned. Then listen and check your answers.

44

a. ◯ Positive and negative aspects about the movie.

b. ◯ His overall opinion about the movie.

c. ◯ A summary of the story.

d. ◯ Name of the director and some of the actors.

3 Listen again and write **T** (true) or **F** (false).

45

a. ◯ The vlogger thinks the movie is perfect.

b. ◯ The story asks big questions about the future.

c. ◯ The story is interesting, but not predictable.

d. ◯ The reviewer doesn't want to see the movie again.

LANGUAGE TIPS

> **Synopsis**: a summary of the story of a movie, book, play etc.
> **Review**: an opinion about a movie, book, play etc.

4 What is the reviewer general opinion about the movie? Go back to activity 1 and color the number of stars that represents his opinion.

5 **Interstellar** depicts a dramatic future of the planet Earth. In groups, write some predictions about this future. How will it be in 2050? Follow the steps below.

a. Get together in groups of four. Decide which aspect of the future you would like to discuss. Examples: environment, technology, medicine, schools, food etc.

b. What is your opinion about this aspect? How do you believe it will be in the future?

c. Look at the previous pages and write down some useful language to support you during the discussion.

d. During the discussion, be respectful with your classmates and their opinions. Here you find some useful language to agree or disagree with them:

- I totally agree with you…
- Yes, you're right. I'm with you!
- Yes, maybe, but I'm not sure…
- I'm sorry, I don't agree.
- Let's agree to disagree.

PRONUNCIATION CORNER

1 Listen and act out the jazz chant.

46

Who is she?
She is Sophie.
Where does she live?
She lives in Athens.

What does she like?
She likes cats.
What does she practice?
She practices yoga.

Sophie has a secret.
Sophie loves movies.
She watches comedies and dramas,
Musicals and thrillers,

Romance and horror films…
Sci-fi and documentaries, too.
She wants to be an actress,
A famous movie actress!

SOPHIE

Nik Neves/Arquivo da editora

2 Read the chart and complete it with other verbs. Then, in pairs, practice the pronunciation of the ending sounds of the verbs in the 3rd person singular (*Simple Present*).

47

Verbs ending in *p, t, k, f, gh, ph* have the /s/ sound in the 3rd person singular.	Verbs ending in *b, d, g, l, m, n, ng, r, v* or with vowel have the /z/ sound in the 3rd person singular.	Verbs ending in *c, s, x, z, ss, ch, sh, ge* have the /iz/ sound in the 3rd person singular.
Stop – sto**ps**	Open – ope**ns**	Miss – miss**es**
_____	_____	_____

READ AND WRITE

Text 1

1 Look at the picture below. What do you know about the movie **Incredibles 2**?

_____

_____

2 Do you usually read a review before watching a movie? Why (not)?

_____

_____

3 Where can you find movie reviews?

_____

_____

4 Read the movie review and check the sentences that are true about **Incredibles 2**.

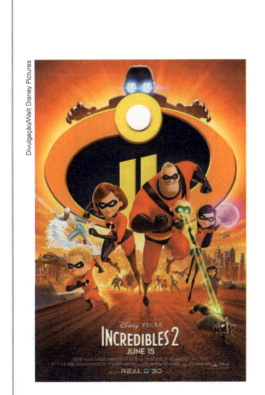

https://www.imdb.com/review/rw4373203/?ref_=tt_urv

 7/10

Incredibles 2 is... Exciting and Acceptable.

NarnialsAwesome   2 October 2018

"Incredibles 2" was probably the most anticipated movie of the year; it's hard to believe it's made 14 years since the first original. So obviously everyone was more than ready for this.

The film does come through when it comes to entertaining action and comedy, with Jack-Jack, Bob, and Edna providing most of the biggest laughs. The plot is interesting, because we've got to know what happened to the Parr family. As far as the supervillain mystery, it's acceptable and somewhat entertaining, but a bit predictable and generic. The final criticism I have is that Edna definitely deserved more screen time.

That being said, it is still an entertaining movie and not at all "painful" to watch.

In conclusion, "Incredibles 2" is funny, exciting, and really worth a viewing.

Available at: <www.imdb.com/review/rw4373203/?ref_=tt_urv>. Accessed on: Mar. 12, 2019.

a. ◯ The original **Incredibles** is from 2004.

b. ◯ The reviewer thinks it is very hard to predict what is going to happen to the supervillain.

c. ◯ In the reviewer's opinion, Edna doesn't appear in a fair number of scenes.

d. ◯ The reviewer believes that some parts of the movie are terrible, and you won't want to watch it.

5 Read some fragments of the movie review in activity 4 and answer the questions.

"The film does come through when it comes to entertaining action and comedy [...]"

"The plot is interesting, because we've got to know what happened to the Parr family [...]"

"[...] it's acceptable and somewhat entertaining, but a bit predictable and generic."

"In conclusion, 'Incredibles 2' is funny, exciting, and really worth a viewing."

a. By reading these fragments, do you think the review is positive or negative?

_____

b. Which adjectives can prove your previous answer?

_____

6 In pairs, reflect on the following questions and answer them.

a. Why do people read movie reviews?

_____

b. Does the reviewer express his opinion? If so, copy an excerpt from the text that proves your answer.

_____

_____

c. Besides movie reviews, what can people read to find out about a movie plot?

_____

7 Do you think that a person who has not watched **Incredibles 2** yet would like to watch it? Why (not)?

_____

_____

Text 2

8 Skim the text below and answer the questions.

a. Does the text belong to the same genre as the one on page 123?

_____

b. In pairs, discuss: what kind of information do you expect to find in the text below?

_____

_____

9 Now, read the text attentively and check **yes** or **no**.

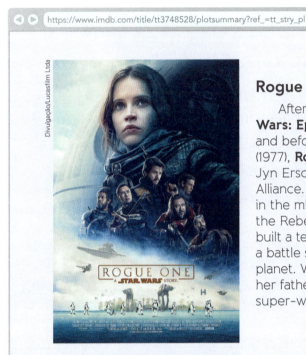

https://www.imdb.com/title/tt3748528/plotsummary?ref_=tt_stry_pl

Divulgação/Lucasfilm Ltda

Rogue One

After the rise of the Galactic Empire in **Star Wars: Episode III – Revenge of the Sith** (2005) and before the Battle of Yavin in **Star Wars** (1977), **Rogue One** (2016) follows the outcast Jyn Erso and how she came to join the Rebel Alliance. Joining the Alliance, Jyn finds herself in the middle of the ultimate conflict between the Rebels and the Empire: her father Galen has built a terrifying super-weapon: The Death Star, a battle station capable of destroying an entire planet. Will Jyn and the Rebels be able to save her father from the Empire and cripple their super-weapon, or will it be too late?

—Johnny

Available at: <www.imdb.com/title/tt3748528/plotsummary?ref_=tt_stry_pl>. Accessed on: Mar. 12, 2019.

	Yes	No
a. Does Rogue One tell the story between Episode III and IV (from 1977)?		
b. Does Jyn Erso fight a major battle between the Empire and the Rebels?		
c. Does Jyn Erso also build a powerful weapon?		
d. Is the The Death Star a terrifying planet?		

10 Answer the questions.

a. Which expression is used in the plot summary to refer to the Death Star?

_____

b. Does the plot summary present the casting list?

_____

c. Who is the character Jyn? How important does this character seem to be?

_____

d. Does the text contain any spoilers? If so, rewrite the excerpt which proves your answer.

_____

11 What about publishing some plot summaries on the school website or blog? Follow the
189   steps below.

a. In pairs, choose a movie that you both like and do some research on the movie plot.

b. Look for a picture to illustrate your plot summary.

c. Write a draft and ask your teacher for correction.

d. Make sure to collect relevant information to mention in your plot summary.

e. Do all the necessary adjustments and write the final version.

f. Publish the plot summary on the school website or blog.

_____

_____

_____

_____

_____

_____

_____

_____

_____

_____

_____

_____

TIPS FOR LIFE

Do you think about the future?

1 In pairs, read the sentence and discuss: do you agree with it?

stocklight/Shutterstock

"We need to think of the future and the planet we are going to leave to our children and their children."

(Kofi Annan)

Available at: <www.brainyquote.com/quotes/kofi_annan_386959>. Accessed on: Mar. 12, 2019.

- Now, discuss the questions below.

  a. Are you worried about the environment preservation?

  _____

  b. Thinking about the planet today. What would you do to make planet Earth better in the future?

  _____

  _____

2 Do some research and write in your notebook a list of movies and documentaries about environment preservation. Share your list with your classmates and teacher.

CHECK YOUR PROGRESS	😃	😐	🙁
Movie genres			
Simple Future (will)			
Wh- questions + Simple Future (will)			
Listening			
Speaking			
Reading			
Writing			

Yana Paskova/Getty Images

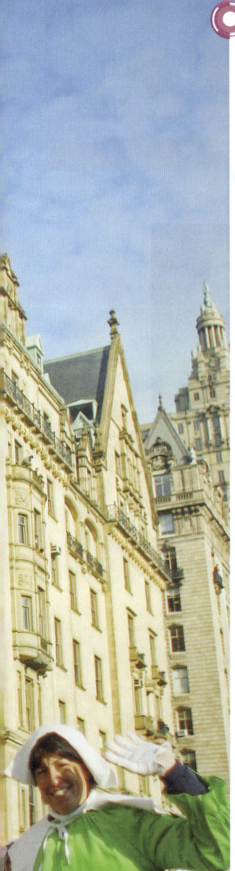

1 Look at the picture and discuss with your classmates.

   a. What are the most important celebrations in your city?

   b. Which one is your favorite? Why?

2 Read and listen to the dialog. Then act out.

48 **John:** Honey, what are we going to do for Thanksgiving this year?

Liz: I was thinking of inviting our parents and Barbara and Harry to join us for dinner. Thanksgiving is a time to give thanks for the bounty on the table and to be grateful for having an opportunity to share a good time with our relatives and friends.

Leo: Oh, that sounds good to me! Thanksgiving is less than two weeks away, isn't it?

Liz: Yes, it is. Thanksgiving is my favorite holiday of the year. It's a time for great enjoyment!

Tobby: I agree. We'll have a big turkey, won't we, Mom?

Liz: Yes, dear. And we'll borrow the big platter from aunt Barbara as usual. She isn't coming, is she?

John: Unfortunately, no, she isn't. She needs to work at the hospital.

Leo: Dad, you're going to make the stuffing, aren't you?

John: Of course I am. It's the best part of the dinner!

Kitty: And I'll make a pumpkin pie.

Tobby: Kitty, I'll eat the whole pie!

John: Tobby, don't be so selfish, there will be eleven of us!

Kitty: What else will we have for dessert, Mom?

Liz: We'll have seasonal fruit.

Tobby: And a big apple pie, too?

Liz: Sure, Tobby! That will be the best Thanksgiving dinner ever.

Everybody: Yeah!!!

3 Read the sentences below and write **T** (true) or **F** (false).

   a. ( ) Liz and John are going to invite their relatives to celebrate Thanksgiving.

   b. ( ) John is going to make a pumpkin pie.

   c. ( ) They will have a big apple pie for dessert.

THINKING AHEAD

1 Observe the picture, read the text, and create a title for it.

www.hello!teens.com/thanksgiving

Thanksgiving Day is a festival celebrated on the fourth Thursday of November in the USA, and on the second Monday of October in Canada. The festival is also celebrated in several other countries around the world, like Australia, Malaysia, India etc. The Thanksgiving celebration originates from the feast held by the Pilgrims and members of the Wampanoag people at Plymouth in 1621, to celebrate their first crop in the new land. Since then, people express gratitude for their blessings and give thanks to dear ones for their love and support. So, families get together to celebrate the day with a special dinner. There are also famous Thanksgiving parades around the world, especially in the USA. The New York Thanksgiving parade is one of the most famous. The way Christmas is celebrated in Brazil is very similar to Thanksgiving once families usually get together around a big meal.

Based on: <www.thanksgiving-day.org>. Accessed on: Feb. 19, 2019.

2 Look at the Thanksgiving Day symbols and number their descriptions.

1   2   3   4

a. ◯ Turkey is a very important part of Thanksgiving family celebration.

b. ◯ Pumpkins have been a Thanksgiving favorite for about 400 years.

c. ◯ Cranberry sauce is turkey's favorite Thanksgiving feast partner.

d. ◯ Corn was part of the first Thanksgiving feast and is still popular nowadays.

1 Listen to the audio about celebrations around the world. Then match the pictures to the
49 sentences.

a. New Year's Day

January 1st

b. Valentine's Day

February 14th

c. International Women's Day

March 8th

d. Thanksgiving Day

Fourth Thursday in November

e. Christmas Day

December 25th

f. St. Patrick's Day in Ireland

March 17th

◯ It celebrates Jesus Christ's birth.

◯ This day honors Saint Patrick.

◯ It was first celebrated by the Pilgrims in 1621.

◯ It celebrates women's rights all over the world.

◯ This celebration begins the night before, when people wish each other a happy and prosperous new year.

◯ It celebrates not only lovers, but also true friendships.

2 Do some research about the celebrations below and write one sentence to describe each one.

a. Easter

_____

b. International Workers' Day

_____

c. Día de los Muertos in Mexico

_____

d. Ouidah Voodoo Festival in Benin

_____

e. Loi Krathong in Thailand

_____

f. Holi in India

_____

3 What is your favorite holiday? Why?

_____

_____

_____

TIME FOR A
GAME

Let's play **Mime, Where are you?** and **Word list!**

1 Read the text below and answer the questions. Then compare the answers in pairs.

| ◀ ▶ | https://www.nordangliaeducation.com/our-schools/bangkok/article/2017/10/31/loi-krathong-festival | _ ☐ ✕ |

| HOME | OUR SCHOOL | OUR STAFF | COMMUNITY | LEARNING | ADMISSIONS | NEWS & EVENTS | CONTACT US |

Loi Krathong Festival

The Loi Krathong festival is a Thai tradition which started a long time ago […]

In Thailand, many people enjoy making their own krathong made from natural resources such as leaves […]. An array of colorful flowers decorate this base […].

Many people strive to float a krathong annually to show their gratitude to the Goddess of the Water […], but also to ask for forgiveness for the pollution we have contributed to the river […]. Some believe that floating a beautiful krathong away in the river also represents the floating away of misfortune […].

A krathong

Boontoom Sae-Kor/Shutterstock

Available at: <www.nordangliaeducation.com/our-schools/bangkok/article/2017/10/31/loi-krathong-festival>. Accessed on: Feb. 21, 2019.

a. What is a krathong made of? _____

b. Why do people float a krathong every year in Thailand?

_____

2 Read the words below. Then look in the text for words that were formed by adding letters to their beginning or ending.

a. fest _____
b. make _____
c. color _____

d. annual _____
e. forgive _____
f. pollute _____

g. beauty _____
h. fortune _____

3 Now complete: a group of specific letters called prefixes and suffixes can be added to the beginning or ending of a word respectively to make…

a. ◯ another word with a different meaning or of a different word class, such as a verb, noun etc.

b. ◯ a synonym or an antonym of the original word.

c. ◯ another word always with the same meaning, but of a different word class.

◀4 Observe the chart and complete the missing information. Use words from the text in activity 1 to give examples.

Prefixes & Suffixes					
Prefixes	**Meaning**	**Example**	**Suffixes**	**Meaning**	**Example**
de-	reverse, change	decrease	**-able**	able to, having the quality of	comfortable
dis-	reverse, opposite, remove	_____appear	**-al**	relating to	_____
im-/il- in-/ir	not	illogical, _____possible, inaction, _____regular	**-ful**	full of	_____ _____
mis-	bad, wrong	_____ misunderstanding	**-ible**	forms adjectives	terrible
mid-	middle	midday	**-sion** **-tion** **-xion**	denoting action or condition	_____
non-	not	_____fiction	**-ly**	forms adverbs and adjectives	_____
un-	against, opposite, not	_____usual	**-less**	without, not affected by	home_____
over-	too much	overcooked	**-y**	full of, denoting a condition	rainy
under-	less than, beneath	_____cooked	**-ness**	denoting a state or condition	_____

◀5 Replace the entire phrase in parentheses with new words you will create using the words in purple and a suffix or a prefix from the box. Write the complete sentences in your notebook. Use a dictionary if needed.

> -ful   -ly   -tion   un-   il-   dis-   mis-

a. It was a (**full of joy**) and (**full of wonder**) dinner.

b. We have a (**every month**) dinner with our uncle.

c. The total (**number of people that populates**) in Brazil is around 210 million people.

d. We were (**not able**) to move on the streets during Carnival.

e. It's (**not legal**) to park here. Move your car, please.

f. I (**do not agree**) with you. I think you are (**not understanding**) me.

Go to page 176.

Some words can be formed by adding a *prefix* and a *suffix* or even *two suffixes* to them. Examples: <u>un</u>happi**ly**, <u>un</u>success**ful**, <u>im</u>possib**ly**, <u>un</u>believ**able**, <u>un</u>break**able**, beauti**fully**, thank**fully**, faith**ful**ness, help**less**ness, use**ful**ness.

6 Bob and Jerry are talking about Bob's memory stick. Read the chart below and complete their dialog with **borrow** or **lend**.

You borrow something from someone.	Someone lends something to you.
Can I **borrow** your music player? Mary **borrowed** 5 dollars from me yesterday.	Dad, can you **lend** me 50 dollars? He is going to **lend** me his bike tomorrow.

Bob: Jerry, did you take my memory stick?

Jerry: No, I didn't. I _____ it from you last Friday, but I returned it on Saturday.
Bob: Oh, yes. That's right!

Jerry: Wait, you _____ it to Lucy last Monday, didn't you?

Bob: You're right. She _____ it from me again...

Jerry: Don't _____ Lucy any of your things. She never gives them back.

7 Read the sentences from the dialog on page 129 paying attention to the highlighted words. Then underline the words and expressions that complete the definitions appropriately.

> Thanksgiving **is** less than two weeks away, **isn't it**?
> We**'ll have** a big turkey, **won't we**, Mom?
> Dad, you**'re going to make** the stuffing, **aren't you**?
> She **isn't** coming, **is she**?

a. The questions at the end of the sentences **confirm the information/request new information**.

b. If we have an affirmative sentence first, the question will be in the **negative/affirmative** form.

c. If we have a negative sentence first, the question will be in the **negative/affirmative** form.

8 Look at the chart about tag questions and complete the gaps with the missing information.

Present (to be)	I am a good guy, aren't I?
	You are Liz's parents, _____ you?
Past (to be)	You were late yesterday, _____ you?
	The movie was good, _____ it?

Present (can)	You can play the keyboard, _____ you?	
	Jane and Lucy can't go to the party, _____ they?	
Past (can)	Before the surgery, she couldn't see well, _____ she?	
Present	Tobby doesn't speak Spanish, _____ he?	
Past	John and Liz didn't buy a new car, _____ they?	
Future	Next year you will travel to Japan, _____ you?	

9 Read the cartoon paying attention to the highlighted words. Then underline the appropriate words in each definition.

a. The highlighted words indicate **actions/ possession/qualities**.

b. They refer to **a noun/a verb/an adjective** that was previously mentioned.

10 Look at the chart and complete the examples with the missing pronouns.

Subject pronouns	Possessive pronouns	Examples
I	Mine	**My pencil** is blue. The blue pencil is _____.
You	Yours	This is **your** present. The present is _____.
He	His	**Bob's** guitar is new. The new guitar is _____.
She	Hers	That's my **mother's** new car. That's _____.
We	Ours	**Tobby and I** bought these tennis balls. They're _____.
You	Yours	**Bill and Ann**, here are your new clothes. They're _____.
They	Theirs	These are **Sam and Ted's** bikes. The bikes are _____.

1 Look at the images from different festivals and celebrations around the world. Then discuss the questions that follow with a classmate.

a. Do you recognize any of these events? Which one(s)?

b. Share what you know about these events: what are their origins? When do they happen? What do they celebrate?

2 Listen to a podcast about these four festivals and celebrations around the world. 50 Look at the images of activity 1 again and match each one to their appropriate name.

a. ⬭ White Nights Festival

b. ⬭ Holi

c. ⬭ Day of the Dead

d. ⬭ Harbin Ice and Snow Festival

3 Listen to the audio again and fill in the chart with information about each festival. 51

Celebration/ Festival	Origin/Place	When	What involves/ celebrates
Harbin Ice and Snow Festival	China	_____ January 5th	_____
Day of the Dead	_____	_____	_____
_____	_____	The end of winter (March)	Love
White Nights Festival	_____	From May to _____	_____

4 Listen to the audio one more time and match the name of each festival with the correct
52 piece of information below.

a. It's an international competition.

b. It includes opera, ballet, and classical music.

c. People get together and forget all resentment.

d. It combines indigenous and catholic traditions.

○ Holi festival

○ White Nights Festival

○ Harbin Ice and Snow Festival

○ Day of the Dead

5 Discuss the following questions with your classmates and teacher.

a. Which celebration do you think is the most interesting? Why?

b. Are there similar celebrations or festivals in Brazil?

PRONUNCIATION CORNER

1 Listen and act out the jazz chant.

53 **A:** Paul doesn't like to study, does he?

B: No, he doesn't.

A: Susan studies hard, doesn't she?

B: No, she doesn't.

A: Tobby won't go to the party, will he?

B: Yes, he will.

A: Sayuri will dance tonight, won't she?

B: Yes, she will.

A + B: Paul doesn't like to study.
Susan doesn't study hard.
Tobby will go to the party.
And Sayuri will dance tonight!

Nik Neves/Arquivo da editora

2 Anne and Denis are talking about music.

54 Listen and practice the dialog paying attention to the **tag questions** intonation.

Anne: Your favorite band is Soul Keepers, isn't it?

Dennis: No, it's not. My favorite band is The Rockers. What about yours?

Anne: Mine? Let me see... The Rescuers is my favorite band.

Dennis: They played at the stadium last night, didn't they?

Anne: Yes, they did. By the way, would you like to borrow my MP3 player to download some of their songs?

Dennis: Sure, I'd love to!

READ AND WRITE

1 The texts below are from the book *Holiday Colors and Lights*, by Stacy McPherson. In your opinion, what is the book about?

◯ Music and food in celebrations and festivities around the world.

◯ Different ways to celebrate Carnival around the world.

◯ The costumes and decorations in celebrations and festivities around the world.

New Year in China

People celebrate holidays around the world with color and light.

Every year, people from China celebrate the New Year. They wear red clothes. They decorate with red paper. Adults give children presents of "lucky money" in red envelopes.

On the last day of Chinese New Year, there is a big festival. Children carry lanterns in parades. Men carry a colorful dragon through the streets.

These New Year traditions are very old. The Chinese celebrated with these same traditions hundreds of years ago.

Holi in India

Every spring, people in India celebrate a holiday called Holi. Holi is a celebration filled with joy and fun. Families dance and sing in the streets. People build large fires to welcome the Holi celebration.

During Holi, people throw colored powder on each other. The powder is traditionally made with flowers. By the end of Holi, colors cover everyone!

2 Read the sentences about the New Year's celebration in China and write **P** (probability) or **F** (fact).

a. ◯ People from all ages wear red in Chinese New Year celebration.

b. ◯ Red is the predominant color during the festivity.

c. ◯ Adults give a special present to children.

d. ◯ Chinese New Year is the major holiday in China.

3 In pairs, answer the questions below.

a. Which expression in the text proves that the Chinese New Year celebration lasts more than one day?

_____

_____

b. Would you like to be part of the Chinese New Year celebration? Why (not)?

_____

_____

4 According to the text about the Holi festival in India, complete the sentences below using the words and expressions from the box.

colorful powder	fun	people from all ages	sing	spring

a. _____ have fun in Holi celebration.

b. Holi is a Hindu _____ festival.

c. Families have a lot of _____ in the streets.

They _____ and dance.

d. People are colored because of a _____ made of flowers.

5 Answer the questions below.

a. What do people do to welcome the Holi celebration?

_____

b. In your opinion, what is the most interesting aspect of the Holi festival?

_____

6 You read about the Chinese New Year and the Holi festival. Now you are going to read about Carnival in Brazil and Loi Krathong in Thailand. Reflect on the question: what is the importance of these festivals and celebrations?

_____

_____

_____

_____

_____

Text 2

7 Read the texts below and do the activities that follow.

Carnival in Brazil

People in Brazil celebrate a big holiday called Carnival. During Carnival, music fills the towns and cities. Brazilians in colorful costumes dance and sing in the streets.

Carnival lasts for almost a week. Thousands of people watch parades during Carnival. Big colorful floats carry dancers and musicians down the streets. It may be the loudest, most colorful party in the world!

Loi Krathong in Thailand

Every November, people in Thailand celebrate a festival of light called Loi Krathong. They light candles in lanterns made from banana leaves. Then they put the lanterns on rivers and watch them drift away.

In one part of Thailand, people don't put lanterns on the water. Instead, they let the lanterns go into the air. The nighttime sky fills with beautiful orange lights.

8 Read the statements about Carnival in Brazil and write **T** (true), **F** (false) or **NM** (not mentioned).

a. ◯ People fill the streets in towns and cities to celebrate Carnival.

b. ◯ Carnival lasts for a weekend.

c. ◯ Carnival is one of the most awaited events in South America.

d. ◯ Floats are small and colorful cars which carry dancers and musicians down the streets.

9 Read the text with information about Loi Krathong and answer.

a. What are the lanterns put on the rivers made from?

_____

b. Do all people in Thailand put the lanterns on the rivers? Explain your answer.

_____

10 Now it is time to create a book of Brazilian festivals and celebrations. Follow the instructions below.

191

- In pairs, choose one festival or celebration from a region in Brazil.

- Do some research and collect pictures about it.

- Take notes of its origin, curiosities, period of celebration, food, music, and dances related to it.

- Write a draft of your text and show it to the teacher. Then do all the necessary adjustments.

- Write or type a final version and glue the pictures to illustrate your text.

- Gather all the texts and create the Book of Brazilian Festivals and Celebrations.

_____

_____

_____

_____

_____

_____

_____

_____

_____

_____

_____

_____

_____

Celebrate our differences

1 Observe the picture, read the quotation and discuss with your classmates.

Rawpixel.com/Shutterstock

"Share our similarities, celebrate our differences."

M. Scott Peck
(American psychiatrist
and best-selling author)

Available at: <www.betterworld.net/quotes/
celebrate-quotes.htm>. Accessed on: Mar. 12, 2019.

a. In your opinion, do these people come from the same place? Why (not)?

_____

_____

b. List two differences and two similarities you identify in them.

_____

_____

c. Read the quotation again and answer: how can you relate this idea to the picture?

_____

_____

2 Break the code and discover M. Scott Peck's message.

1	2	3	4	5	6	7	8	9	10	11	12
A	B	C	D	E	I	L	R	S	T	V	Y

7	5	10	'	9		3	5	7	5	2	8	1	10	5		4	6	11	5	8	9	6	10	12	!

CHECK YOUR PROGRESS	😃	😐	🙁
Holidays			
Prefixes & Suffixes			
Possessive pronouns			
Tag questions			
Listening			
Speaking			
Reading			
Writing			

1 Complete the gaps with the correct form of the future: **will** or **going to**.

a. What time _____ you _____ to bed tonight? (go)

b. I'm afraid I _____ here for your birthday party next Sunday. (be – negative)

c. Tim is sick, so he _____ attending any classes today. (be – negative)

d. I _____ at the school library for my English test. (study)

e. I _____ you with your History homework tonight. (help)

f. Some students _____ the museum next week. (go)

g. It's cold here. I _____ the window. (close)

2 Rewrite the sentences using the correct Possessive Pronouns. Follow the example.

This is my pencil.

This pencil is mine.

a. That is Paula's notebook.

_____

b. Those are Miguel's comic books.

_____

c. These are Tom's and Meg's English books.

_____

d. This is your blue T-shirt.

_____

e. Those are Catherine's documents.

_____

f. This video game belongs to me and my sister.

_____

3 Underline the correct word to complete each sentence.

a. This is your winter coat and that is **her/hers** coat.

b. Is that his dog or is it **her/hers**?

c. **My/Mine** comic book is funnier than **your/yours**.

d. **Her/Hers** house is smaller than **our/ours**.

e. Are these CDs **your/yours** or **my/mine**?

f. I'm going to the movies with **my/mine** friends tonight.

4 Read and check the correct answer.

a. without hope ◯ hopeless ◯ hopeful

b. full of joy ◯ joyless ◯ joyful

c. not happy ◯ happily ◯ unhappy

d. not tidy ◯ tidiness ◯ untidy

e. not able to ◯ unable to ◯ be able to

f. not agree ◯ agree ◯ disagree

5 Complete the dialogs with the sentences from the box.

> You don't have any plans for tomorrow night, do you?
> Do you want to go to the movies with me on Sunday?
> This pen is yours, isn't it?
> Can you lend me your pencil just for a minute?
> You don't like to watch documentaries, do you?

a. **A:** _____

   B: Yes, it's mine.

b. **A:** _____

   B: Sorry, but I'm going to use it now.

c. **A:** _____

   B: No, I don't. Why?

d. **A:** _____

   B: Oh, I'm sorry. On Sunday I need to help my mother.

e. **A:** _____

   B: No, I don't. I prefer musicals.

UNITS 1 AND 2

1 Read an extract from Anne Frank's diary and check the correct answers.

Wednesday, July 7, 1943

[...]

Do You Remember?

Memories of my schooldays at the Jewish Lyceum

Do you remember? I've spent many a delightful hour talking about school, teachers, adventures and boys. Back when our lives were still normal, everything was so wonderful. That one year of Lyceum was heaven to me: the teachers, the things I learned, the jokes, the prestige, the crushes, the admirers.

[...]

Do you remember? How Lies and I told on the class. We had a French test. I wasn't having too much trouble with it, but Lies was. She copied my answers and I went over them to make corrections (on her test, I mean). She got a C+ and I got a C–, since thanks to my help she had gotten some things right, but both grades had been crossed out and replaced with a big fat F. Great indignation. We went to Mr. Premsela to explain what had happened, and at the end Lies said, "Yes, but the entire class had their books open under their desks!". Mr. Premsela promised the class that nobody would be punished if all those who had cheated would raise their hands. About ten hands went up—less than half the class, of course. A few days later Mr. Premsela sprang the test on us again. Nobody would talk to Lies and me, and we were branded as snitches. I soon caved in under the pressure and wrote a long letter of apology to Class 1 L II, begging their forgiveness. Two weeks later all had been forgotten.

[...]

Available at: <www.penguinrandomhouse.ca/books/55525/anne-franks-tales-from-the-secret-annex-by-anne-frank-edited-by-gerrold-van-der-stroom-and-susan-massotty-translated-by-susan-massotty/9780553586381/excerpt>. Accessed on: Mar. 17, 2019.

We know this is a diary entry because...

a. it is written in the ◯ past. ◯ present. ◯ future.

b. it indicates the ◯ address. ◯ e-mail. ◯ date.

c. it narrates what happened ◯ with details. ◯ without details.

2 Read the diary entry again and circle the correct answer.

a. Everything was **wonderful/troubled** when her life was normal.

b. She has **bad/good** memories about her schooldays.

c. The diary entry narrates an episode about **a French test/her crushes**.

d. **Anne Frank/Mr. Premsela** talked to the teacher to explain what had happened.

e. The teacher **didn't punish/punished** Anne's classmates.

3 Read the text again and answer **T** (true) or **F** (false).

a. ( ) Anne's friend copied her answers on the test.

b. ( ) Anne's grade was higher than her friend's grade.

c. ( ) The teacher asked the best students to raise their hands.

d. ( ) The teacher apologized to all the students who cheated.

e. ( ) Anne was upset because the teacher gave another test to everyone again.

4 Read the list below and find in the text a synonym for each of these words.

a. took the place of _____

b. problem _____

c. acted dishonestly or unfairly

_____

d. charming _____

e. passion, admiration _____

f. canceled, deleted _____

5 Read another extract from Anne Frank's diary and do the following activity.

"the first thing I stuck in was this diary, and then curlers, handkerchiefs, schoolbooks, a comb, and some old letters"

Available at: <http://time.com/4770800/anne-frank-secret-annex/>. Accessed on: Mar. 17, 2019.

Write a text about what you would take in your bag if you had to hide for a long time. Explain the reasons why you would take such things.

_____

_____

_____

_____

_____

_____

_____

EXTRA PRACTICE

UNITS 3 AND 4

1 Read the following text and check the correct answer.

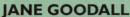

https://kids.britannica.com/kids/article/Jane-Goodall/353195

JANE GOODALL

Stephen Robinson/Photoshot/AGB Photo Library

The British scientist Jane Goodall is known for her research on **chimpanzees**. She studied the animals for many years in the East African country of **Tanzania**. Her discoveries changed the way chimpanzees are studied and understood.

Jane Goodall was born on April 3, 1934, in London, England. At a young age she became interested in animals. By age 11 she dreamed of living among Africa's wildlife.

[...]

In 1960 Goodall set up camp on the shores of Tanzania's **Lake Tanganyika**. She studied chimpanzees close-up in their natural setting. It took months for Goodall to gain the chimps' trust, but her patience paid off.

Through her observations, Goodall changed many ideas about chimpanzees. She saw a chimpanzee make a tool, which it used to get food. Scientists had believed only humans were toolmakers. She also found that chimpanzees eat both meat and plants. Finally, Goodall observed that each chimpanzee had a distinct personality and emotions.

Except for short absences, Goodall remained in Tanzania until 1975. In 1977 she founded the Jane Goodall Institute for Wildlife Research, Education, and Conservation.

Did You Know?
The tool that Goodall saw chimps making was a stick that they used to pull termites from a mound.

United Archives GmbH/Alamy/Fotoarena

Available at: <https://kids.britannica.com/kids/article/Jane-Goodall/353195>. Accessed on: Mar. 19, 2019.

This text is a…

a. ◯ biography entry. **b.** ◯ letter. **c.** ◯ news report.

2 Read the text again and match the questions to their corresponding answers.

a. Who is this biography about? ◯ By observing their behavior.

b. What is her nationality? ◯ She is British.

c. What was her research about? ◯ It's about Jane Goodall.

d. How did she change the ideas about chimpanzees? ◯ She studied chimpanzees in their natural habitat.

e. Where did she study the chimpanzees? ◯ It was about chimpanzees.

3 Read the text once more and write the date of each event described in the following statements.

a. She set up camp in Tanzania. _____

b. She left Tanzania. _____

c. She founded the Jane Goodall Institute for Wildlife Research, Education, and

Conservation. _____

d. She was born in London, England. _____

4 Read the text one more time and check **Right**, **Wrong** or **Not mentioned**.

a. Jane's research changed the way people study and understand chimpanzees.

◯ Right ◯ Wrong ◯ Not mentioned

b. Dr. Goodall's favorite chimpanzee is still David, the very first one that trusted her.

◯ Right ◯ Wrong ◯ Not mentioned

c. Chimpanzees only eat plants.

◯ Right ◯ Wrong ◯ Not mentioned

d. Dr. Goodall was sometimes not patient with the fact that she had to wait until the animals started to trust her.

◯ Right ◯ Wrong ◯ Not mentioned

e. Scientists concluded that humans are the only ones who can build tools.

◯ Right ◯ Wrong ◯ Not mentioned

5 What other animal activists do you know? Write a short text about a person you admire for being an animal activist. Describe the actions this person takes to protect animals and then share your thoughts with your teacher and classmates.

_____

_____

UNITS 5 AND 6

1 Read the infographic and check the correct answer. What is it about?

Available at: <https://sites.google.com/site/sportsinschoolareverybenficial/counterclaims>.
Accessed on: Mar. 19, 2019.

It is about...

a. ◯ academic performance in Physics and Science.

b. ◯ the advantages of being physically active for children.

c. ◯ the different routines in schools.

2 Read the infographic again and answer the following questions using the correct information.

a. Number of children who don't practice sports nowadays: _____

b. Number of hours practicing physical activity children need per day: _____

c. Number of hours per day children spend in front of a screen: _____

3 Read the infographic once more. Then read the questions and check the correct answers.

a. What happens to children with lower levels of physical fitness?

○ They have higher grades.

○ They have lower grades.

b. What does the author mean by "screen"?

○ By "screen", the author means "TV, video games, and computer".

○ By "screen", the author means "interactive whiteboard".

c. What is improved by physical activities?

○ Academic performance, attendance, and behavior.

○ The increase of the number of hours spent in front of a screen.

4 The words listed below were extracted from the infographic. Read it once again and pay attention to the context of each word. Then match the words to their meanings.

a. behavior

b. attendance

c. fitness

d. twice

e. poor

f. level

○ The condition of a person being physically fit and healthy.

○ The way through which a person acts.

○ Two times; on two occasions.

○ Being present at a place or event.

○ A position on a real or imaginary scale of amount.

○ Not good or operating well, or of a low quality or standard.

5 Are you physically active? Think about your habits and routine and write a list of actions you take daily to be physically active. Would you say your habits are healthy or would you like to improve them? Discuss it with your teacher and classmates.

_____

_____

_____

_____

_____

_____

_____

_____

_____

EXTRA PRACTICE

UNITS 7 AND 8

1 Read the text and check the correct answer. What is it about?

https://www.littlethings.com/

7 Ways That 'The Jetsons' Accurately Predicted The Future

by GRACE EIRE

Back in 1962, when the cartoon *The Jetsons* first aired on TVs across the nation, everything about it seemed like it came from a very far and distant future.

From the flying cars to the robot maids and conveyor belts that moved humans so they'd never have to walk again, this world seemed like it would only ever exist in the imagination. [...]

Yet, just over half a decade later, are many unmistakable similarities between the technologies on the show and those in our current day-to-day lives. [...]

1. Flat Screens

The screens throughout the Jetson household are much, much slimmer than the TV sets that existed back in 1962. They are not too far off from what our ultra-thin LCD TVs look like today.

2. The Internet

The Jetsons family had access to all sorts of information at the tips of their fingers. If that's not modern-day Internet, I don't know what is!

3. Tiny Cameras That Look Inside You

A lot of the technology on *The Jetsons* leaned on the smaller side, or, rather, the tiny side. [...] There were little cameras that they would swallow for checkups performed from the inside.

4. Screens You Wear On Your Wrist

With all of the exercise watches and even watches that you can text on, the Jetsons definitely predicted this one correctly. [...]

5. Telecommunication

Family members talk to each other through their TVs and other screens all the time on the show, which isn't at all unlike the video-calling services we use on our phones and computers each and every day.

6. Helpful Robots

[...] Well, today we have a few different little robots that help us throughout the day, including interactive maps and

GPS on our phones that talk to us, software on our phones that will answer our questions when we address them by name, and the same name-activated technology for our homes. [...]

7. Meals At The Touch Of A Button

Vending machines are just the start of it, as ordering food online has become easier than ever. All you have to do is click "order" and you will have food in front of you in 30 minutes. On top of that, though, food is even being made on 3D printers, so you literally just have to press "print" and your food is created before your eyes. [...]

Available at: <www.littlethings.com/jetsons-predict-the-future/4>. Accessed on: Mar. 19, 2019.

It is about…

a. ◯ the future of *The Jetsons*.

b. ◯ people who can predict the future.

c. ◯ *The Jetsons'* predictions for the future.

2 Read the text again and circle the correct option.

a. The Jetsons had things that **didn't exist/existed** at that time.

b. They had **diesel/flying** cars.

c. The Jetsons had access to a kind of **internet/air conditioning**.

d. They talked to each other through the **TV/telephone**.

e. There **wasn't/was** a device with a screen that they wore on their wrists.

3 Read the text once more and match the questions to the correct answers.

a. When was *The Jetsons* launched?

b. Did they have video calling at that time?

c. How did they use to cook their meals?

d. Who helped them with the daily housework?

e. Did they have a popular TV set from 1962?

○ A robot maid.

○ No, they didn't. They had a flat screen TV set.

○ They just had to press a button.

○ Yes, they did.

○ Back in 1962.

4 Read the text one more time. Then check the objects we use nowadays which are similar to the ones that appear in *The Jetsons*.

a.
Syda Productions/Shutterstock

c.
Dmitry Kalinovsky/Shutterstock

e.
Denys Prykhodov/Shutterstock

b.
dantess/Shutterstock

d.
Quality Stock Arts/Shutterstock

f.
Rocketclips, Inc./Shutterstock

5 What are your predictions for the future? Imagine you are a sci-fi writer and you have to think about what kind of things are going to be created in the future. Write three examples of the future appliances and describe their function and design.

_____

_____

_____

_____

_____

PROJECT 1

REMARKABLE PEOPLE BIOGRAPHIES

1 This is a picture of Aaron Fotheringham, who is considered a remarkable person. Look at the image and talk to your classmates about it. Then answer the questions below.

Mike Ray/Barcroft USA/Getty Images

a. Have you heard about Aaron Fotheringham before?

_____

b. Why do you think he is considered a remarkable person?

_____

c. In your opinion, why are some people recognized as being remarkable? What do you think they did to receive this label?

_____

d. Do you think the world needs more remarkable people? Why (not)?

_____

2 Now read a small biography of Aaron Fotheringham. Then answer the questions.

https://www.sunrisemedical.co.uk/

Aaron Fotheringham

In addition to being one of the most inspirational disabled celebrities, Aaron Fotheringham is also one of the most famous skaters in the world. His speciality? Wheelchair skating.

During his childhood, Aaron underwent several failed hip operations that forced him to use a wheelchair permanently. Even so, he continued to practice a sport which he was passionate about adapting to his disability.

In 2005, Aaron Fotheringham landed a great jump with a 180° turn, and in 2006 made the first somersault in wheelchair history. Since then, his achievements and challenges are an example for thousands of people.

Available at: <www.sunrisemedical.co.uk/blog/famous-people-with-disabilities>. Accessed on: Mar. 17, 2019.

a. Skim the text. Then search in the dictionary for the words which meaning you still don't know.

_____

b. Which part of Aaron Fotheringham's biography did you consider more interesting? Explain your answer.

_____

c. How can a biography contribute to people's lives or to society as a whole?

_____

3 Read the biography of a remarkable Mexican artist. Then write **T** (true) or **F** (false) for the sentences below.

https://www.sunrisemedical.co.uk/

Frida Kahlo

Frida suffered polio during her childhood and, according to some sources, also had spina bifida, which caused dysmetria in her right leg. In addition, her spinal problems were aggravated by an accident suffered in her adolescence, which left her with physical issues for her entire life.

Frida spent much of her life in bed suffering from severe pain. Even so, she became one of the most famous artists of all time and an icon of the twentieth century.

Lucas Vallecillos / Alamy/Fotoarena

Available at: <www.sunrisemedical.co.uk/blog/famous-people-with-disabilities>. Accessed on: Mar. 17, 2019.

○ The text exposes all moments of Frida's life.

○ The text is a summary of Frida's life.

○ By reading the text, we can understand why Frida is considered a remarkable person.

4 Now it's your turn to create small biographies of remarkable people. Follow the instructions from your teacher and hands on!

_____

_____

_____

_____

_____

_____

_____

_____

_____

FESTIVALS AND CELEBRATIONS

1 Look at the picture below and answer the questions.

Bill Heinsohn/Getty Images

a. What can you see in the picture?

_____

_____

b. This is a picture of a celebration. Do you know which one is it?

_____

_____

c. Which elements of the picture show it was probably taken in a festival or celebration? Explain.

_____

_____

2 Read the text about the Albuquerque International Ballon Fiesta. Then answer the questions.

Albuquerque International Balloon Fiesta

This annual festival of hot air balloons has become so huge in the past few years that I could not contain myself from including it in this list. If you have the opportunity to visit Albuquerque, New Mexico, during early October, you will have the chance to witness a beautiful and colorful scene of thousands of hot air balloons ascending into the sky. The Fiesta continues for nine days, and you can enjoy various musical performances, see "night glows" in which the balloons' propane burners are ignited, but the hot air balloons are tethered to the ground. One of the best events at the festival is the Mass Ascension where hundreds of hot air balloons are launched in two waves and fill up the sky with bright colors.

Available at: <www.praguepost.com/travel/best-festivals-around-the-world>. Accessed on: Mar. 20, 2019.

a. Now that you know what the festival is about, write two of its characteristics according to the text.

_____

_____

b. In your opinion, why is this festival important to people?

_____

_____

3 Now you are going to produce a podcast about a festival or celebration and present it to your classmates. Follow the instructions your teacher is going to give you and hands on.

_____

_____

_____

_____

_____

_____

_____

_____

_____

_____

◀1 Complete the chart using the words from the box and match them to the pictures. Then add two more examples of your own. Use a dictionary to help you.

cab	chips	cinema	flashlight	flat	football	gas
mobile phone		pants	sneakers	theater	underground	

Ilustrações: Olavo Costa/Arquivo da editora; Bandeiras: Banco de imagens/Arquivo da editora

	🇺🇸	🇬🇧
1		taxi
2	soccer	
3	cell phone	
4		trousers
5	movie theater	
6		trainers
7		theatre
8	subway	
9	(French) fries	
10		torch
11		petrol
12	apartment	
13		
14		

a. ◯   e. ◯   i. ◯

b. ◯   f. ◯   j. ◯

c. ◯   g. ◯   k. ◯

d. ◯   h. ◯   l. ◯

2 Find six words related to remarkable people in the word search. Then write one or two sentences using them.

R	I	C	H	A	L	L	E	N	G	E	T	P	H
G	O	J	F	R	I	D	G	E	C	I	L	E	U
B	E	A	C	T	I	V	I	S	T	S	E	C	M
P	R	F	D	D	U	K	E	C	I	T	A	A	A
R	P	E	Y	W	A	Z	L	A	F	J	K	M	N
I	C	O	E	T	D	L	E	E	H	O	N	E	I
G	R	P	H	J	M	Q	K	A	A	P	L	B	T
H	A	S	P	R	I	Z	E	P	L	M	M	A	A
T	C	W	U	J	R	L	S	B	O	O	N	L	R
S	B	M	H	H	E	L	P	T	G	I	L	L	I
N	C	S	D	R	I	I	O	T	O	V	N	M	A
Q	T	T	C	E	L	L	N	L	K	F	D	Q	N

_____

_____

3 Check the correct sentences related to the following pictures.

PICTURE 1

PICTURE 2

○ The city in picture 1 is colder than in picture 2.

○ The city in picture 2 is more polluted than the city in picture 1.

○ The pace of life in picture 2 is faster than the pace of life in picture 1.

○ The city in picture 1 is bigger than the city in picture 2.

○ The city in picture 1 is calmer than the city in picture 2.

FUN ACTIVITIES 2

1 Unscramble the words and complete the crossword. Then identify the body parts in the picture according to the items below.

a. ethra _____

b. irban _____

c. klaen _____

d. dlusohre _____

e. slmuesc _____

f. mahotsc _____

g. aedh _____

h. neke _____

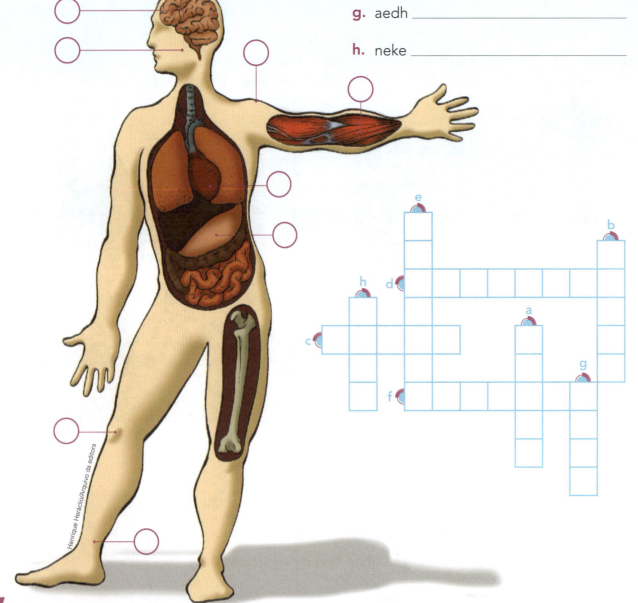

Henrique Herácio/Arquivo da editora

2 Match the movie genres to their definitions. Then number the movie posters below.

1. Action   **3.** Comedy   **5.** Drama   **7.** Romance   **9.** Horror

2. Animation   **4.** Documentary **6.** Musical   **8.** Science fiction **10.** War

◯ This kind of movie is imaginative. It usually includes spaceships, aliens or monsters.

◯ This kind of movie is written based on a historical event or history.

◯ This kind of movie sets in battles and wars. It's usually about historical events.

◯ This kind of movie has many songs and dance performances.

◯ This kind of movie usually has shocking or scary scenes to frighten people.

◯ This kind of movie is created using drawings. The story is usually about animated objects, animals with human characteristics and funny adventures.

◯ This kind of movie usually has stunts, fights, high energy scenes and special effects.

◯ This kind of movie usually exaggerates the situations, characters and language to provoke laughter.

◯ This kind of movie is about love and relationships. It usually presents a touching story.

◯ This kind of movie usually presents emotional stories of people going through conflicts.

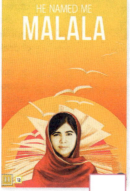

GLOSSARY

A

aboard: a bordo de
above: acima de
abroad: no exterior, em outro país
acknowledgement: reconhecimento
acquaintance: conhecido/a
across: através; de um lado para outro
actually: realmente; na verdade
affluence: boa situação financeira
affordable: de preço acessível
afraid: com medo
after: após, depois de
against: contra
ago: atrás (tempo)
agree: concordar
aileron: peça situada na asa dos aviões, que controla o eixo de rotação
aircraft: aeronave
alive: vivo/a
all night long: a noite toda
all over: por toda parte
allow: permitir
almost: quase
along: por, ao longo de
already: já
although: embora, apesar de
amazing: espantoso/a, incrível
among: entre (vários)
amount: quantidade
angry: zangado/a
another: outro/a
ant: formiga
any: algum/a; qualquer
anything: qualquer coisa
appointment: compromisso, consulta
argue: argumentar, discutir
as: como; tão
as soon as: o quanto antes
ashamed: envergonhado/a
astonish: surpreender
at: em, no/a; (horas) às
augmentation: aumento
aunt: tia
average: média
avoid: evitar

award: prêmio
awareness: conscientização
away: longe
awesome: muito legal, bárbaro/a
awkward: esquisito/a

B

back: costas; atrás
backward: para trás
bad: mau/má
bake: assar
barely: quase não
bat: morcego
B&B: (bed and breakfast) hospedagem que oferece quarto e café da manhã
be able to: ser capaz de
bee: abelha
before: antes
behave: comportar-se
believe: acreditar
bell: campainha; sino
belt: cinto
bench: banco, assento
berries: pequenas frutas vermelhas (amora, framboesa, etc.)
beside: ao lado de
best: o/a melhor
better: melhor que
between: entre (duas coisas, pessoas, etc.)
billboard: painel, cartaz
birth: nascimento
bit: pouco/a
bite: morder; mordida
blank: lacuna
blanket: cobertor
blast: explosão
bless: abençoar
blood: sangue
blood vessel: vaso sanguíneo
bloom: desabrochar
blush: ruborizar-se; rubor
boat: barco
boiled: cozido/a
bond: vincular; laço, vínculo
booking: reserva (de estadia)
border: divisa
born: nascido/a
borrow: tomar emprestado/a

bottleneck: estreitamento, demora, gargalo, engarrafamento
bought: comprou
bound: limite, fronteira
bountiful: farto/a
bounty: abundância; generosidade
bow: curvar, fazer uma reverência
bowl: tigela
brake: freio
break: quebrar; intervalo
break down: separar
breakfast: café da manhã
breathe: respirar
breathtaking: de tirar o fôlego
bright: brilhante, claro
brittle: frágil
broke: quebrou
brought: trouxe
brush: escovar; escova
buckle: fivela
building: edifício
bully: usar superioridade física para intimidar pessoas mais fracas
bunch: monte
bunker: fugitivo/a; abrigo
bureau: escritório
burn: queimar; queimadura
busy: ocupado/a
butterfly: borboleta
button: botão
buzzer: buzina
by: de; por

C

came: veio
candle: vela
canned: enlatado/a
capsaicin: elemento encontrado em pimentas do tipo chili
caption: legenda
care: cuidado
careful: cuidadoso/a
carry: carregar
cast: elenco
cattle: gado bovino
celery: aipo
chain: acorrentar; corrente
challenge: desafio

change: mudar, trocar
charge: cobrar; taxa
check-in: apresentação de bilhete de viagem para embarque
chest: peito
choice: escolha
chowder: caldo feito com peixe e frutos do mar
church: igreja
cider: sidra; suco de maçã
clam: molusco comestível
clap: aplaudir
clear: esclarecer, clarear; claro
(to) clear off: cair fora
clerk: funcionário/a
clever: esperto/a, inteligente
climb: subir, escalar
close: fechar; perto
clothes: roupas
cloud: nuvem
clumsy: desajeitado/a
coach: orientador/a
collarbone: clavícula
college: faculdade
come out: sair
compelling: convincente
control paddle: controle de *videogame*
convey: levar
conveyor belt: esteira de bagagem
cook: cozinhar; cozinheiro/a
cookie: bolacha; biscoito
cool: esfriar; legal
corn: milho
corner: canto, esquina
cottage: chalé
could: podia, poderia
country: país
couple: casal, par
cousin: primo/a
craft: artesanato
cranberry: oxicoco, mirtilo vermelho (fruta)
crash: bater, chocar-se
crazy: louco/a
cripple: paralisar
crop: colheita; plantação
crossbreed: híbrido/a
crowded: cheio/a, lotado/a
crude: bruto/a
cushion: almofada

D

damage: danificar; dano
damp: úmido/a
danger: perigo
dark: escuro/a
darkness: escuridão
date: namorar; data
deal: acordo
decimated: dizimado/a
deep: profundo/a
default: descuido, omissão
defy: desafiar
degree: grau
delight: encantar; encanto
descend: aterrisar, descer
desk: carteira, escrivaninha
dessert: sobremesa
dig up: desenterrar
dingo: cachorro selvagem
disability: deficiência
disease: doença
dish: prato
dispatcher: despachante
done: feito/a
donor: doador/a
doorbell: campainha
dot: ponto
dotted: repleto; pontilhado
drag: força de resistência
drain: esvaziar
draw: desenhar
dream: sonhar; sonho
drew: desenhou
dried: seco/a
drift off: adormecer aos poucos
drop: baixar altitude, deixar cair; gota, pingo
dryer: secadora de roupas
dying: morrendo

E

early age: idade precoce
emperor: imperador
employee: empregado/a
employment: emprego
enable: capacitar, possibilitar
enhance: acentuar, destacar
enjoy: divertir-se
enlighten: esclarecer
entertainment: divertimento
entirely: inteiramente
even: mesmo
evenly: uniformemente
ever: sempre; alguma vez; já
everybody: todo mundo
everything: tudo
excel: destacar-se, sobressair

exchange: trocar
exciting: animador, empolgante
expectancy: expectativa
eye: olho

F

fabric: tecido
fair: feira
fair play: jogo limpo
faith: fé
fall in love: apaixonar-se
famine: fome
fanciful: extravagante
farewell: adeus, despedida
farm: fazenda
fashionable: que segue a moda, elegante
fasten: fechar bem, apertar
feast: festa
feature: recurso, característica
fee: taxa
feel: sentir
few: poucos
field: campo
fight: lutar
fill: encher
find: achar
fingernail: unha da mão
fingertip: ponta do dedo
fireworks: fogos de artifício
fit: encaixar, servir
fix: consertar
flag: bandeira
flee: fugir
float: flutuar
floor: piso; andar
flour: farinha
folder: pasta
folding: dobrável
follow: seguir
foot: pé
forecast: previsão
foreign: estrangeiro/a
forget: esquecer
former: antigo/a, primeiro/a, ex
forth: adiante, à frente
forward: para a frente
fowl: ave, galinha
frame: moldura; quadro
freeze: congelar
freight: frete; carga
fried: frito/a
fuel: combustível
fully: completamente
furnish: mobiliar
furniture: mobília
further: mais distante
furthermore: além disso

G

gadget: dispositivo
gap: lacuna
gave: deu
genre: gênero
gentleman: cavalheiro
get around: contornar
gift: presente; dom
glad: contente
glass: vidro; copo
gliding: voo livre
glue: colar; cola
golden: de ouro, dourado/a
goodies: petiscos, delícias
gosh: Nossa!, Puxa!
gossip: fofoca
got: conseguiu
grab: pegar, apanhar
grasp: agarrar
gratefulness: gratidão
gravy: molho de carne
great: grande, ótimo/a
greet: cumprimentar
ground: solo, chão
grow: crescer
grown-up: adulto/a
growth: crescimento
guess: adivinhar; palpite
guest: convidado/a
guy: rapaz

H

half (halves): metade/ metades
handcraft: trabalho manual
handsome: bonito
hanging: pendurado/a
harm: causar dano
harmful: prejudicial
harvest: colheita, safra
hate: detestar, odiar; ódio
hazardous: perigoso/a
headline: manchete
heal: curar
health: saúde
hear: ouvir
heat: calor
heavy: pesado/a
hell: inferno
help: ajudar; ajuda
hill: colina
hit: atingir; sucesso
hold: segurar; abraçar
homage: homenagem
honey: mel; querido/a
honor: homenagear; honra
horn: chifre; trompa (instrumento)
host: anfitrião/anfitriã
housekeeping: trabalho doméstico
however: no entanto

hug: abraçar; abraço
huge: enorme
hummingbird: beija-flor
hungry: com fome, faminto
hurtful: ofensivo/a
husband: marido

I

ice: gelo
if: se
impregnable: impenetrável
improve: melhorar
increasing: crescente
indeed: de fato; certamente
ineffectual: ineficaz
in-line: alinhado/a
inside: dentro de
instead: em vez de
intend: pretender
into: para dentro de
introduce: apresentar
iron: passar roupa; ferro
isle: ilhota

J

jail: prisão
jewel: pedra preciosa; joia
jewelry: joias, joalheria
job: trabalho
joke: piada
journey: viagem; jornada
joyous: alegre
juice: suco
just: acabar de; só, somente

K

keyboard: teclado
kid: brincar; criança
kinetic: cinético/a; relativo a movimento
kingdom: reino
knife: faca
knock: bater
knowledge: conhecimento

L

labor: trabalho
lack: falta
land: aterrissar; terra
landfill: aterro sanitário
landing: pouso
landscape: paisagem; panorama; vista
last: último/a
late: atrasar; atrasado/a
laugh: rir; risada

laughably: ridículo/a, absurdo/a
laureate: contemplado/a; honrado/a
lead: guiar; liderar
learn: aprender
least: o menos
leave: deixar
led: conduziu, levou
left: deixou; esquerdo/a
lend: emprestar
length: comprimento
less: menos
let: deixar
let's: vamos
lever: alavanca; ação de levantar
library: biblioteca
lifespan: expectativa de vida
lifestyle: estilo de vida
lift: levantar; elevador; elevação
lightbulb: lâmpada
litter: lixo
live: morar, viver
lively: vivo/a, animado/a
load: carregar; carga
look like: parecer-se com
lot: porção
(a) lot of: muito/a
lots of: muitos/as
lounge: salão
lower: mais baixo/a
lowered: abaixado/a
lucky: sortudo/a
lush: exuberante
lyrics: letra de música

maid: empregada doméstica
main: principal
major: principal; muito importante
make over: reformar, redecorar
managed: gerenciado/a
married: casado/a
mash: amassar
mashed potatoes: purê de batatas
mastering: especializado/a
masterpiece: obra-prima
match: combinar, ligar
matter: problema; assunto
may: poder (permissão, possibilidade)
maybe: talvez
meal: refeição
mean: significar, querer dizer
measure: medir, medida
meat: carne
melt: derreter
met: encontrou

mining: mineração
mirror: espelho
miss: sentir falta de
mistake: erro
mix: misturar
moreover: além disso
most: mais
much: muito
muscle: músculo
Muslim: muçulmano/a
must: precisar, ter de

nasty: desagradável
need: precisar; necessidade
neighbor: vizinho/a
netetiquette: netiqueta (conduta para comunicação cordial on-line)
networking: rede
news: notícias
newspaper: jornal
next: próximo/a
nobody: ninguém
noise: barulho
noon: meio-dia
nothing: nada
now: agora
nowadays: hoje em dia

o'clock: hora exata
odd: estranho/a
officer: funcionário/a; oficial
often: frequentemente
oily: oleoso/a
okey-dokey: que legal!
ongoing: em andamento
onion: cebola
only: somente
open: abrir; aberto
order: ordem; pedido
out: fora
outside: do lado de fora, lá fora
overlapping: sobreposição
overtake: substituir
overview: visão geral
overwhelmed: sobrecarregado/a
owe: dever (algo)
own: próprio/a
owner: proprietário/a

paddle: remo
pamper: mimar
parade: desfile, parada
pardon: desculpe, perdão
parent: pai ou mãe

parking lot: estacionamento
parliament: parlamento
partner: parceiro/a, sócio/a
party pooper: desmancha--prazeres
pattern: padrão
peak: pico
pepper: pimenta
perform: apresentar-se
perhaps: talvez
perspiration: transpiração
picky: exigente
pie: torta
piece: pedaço
pilgrim: peregrino/a
pimple: espinha
pin: alfinete
pitch: arremesso
pity: pena, dó
platter: travessa
playtime: momento para diversão
plenty: bastante
plot: enredo, trama
plum: ameixa
plunge: queda repentina, mergulho
plus: mais
poisonous: venenoso/a
pool: apanhado, associação
pork chops: costeletas de porco
previously: anteriormente
prize: prêmio
probe: investigar, indagar
procedure: procedimento
propeller: hélice, propulsor
pull: puxar
pump: bombear; bomba
pumpkin: abóbora
pumpkin patch: plantação de abóbora
puppetry: teatro de marionetes
pursuit: busca
push: empurrar
put: pôr, colocar

quaint: estranho/a
quickly: rapidamente
quirky: peculiar
quiz show: programa de perguntas de cultura geral
quote: citação

rabbit: coelho
rainbow: arco-íris
rainforest: floresta tropical
raise: criar; subir; levantar; sustentar
rang: tocou

range: extensão, alcance
rate: classificação
rather: preferivelmente
(I'd) rather be: eu preferiria ser/estar
reach: alcançar
ready: pronto/a
realize: perceber
rear: parte de trás
reign: reinado
released: lançado/a
reliable: confiável
relief: alívio
remain: permanecer
remained: manteve-se
remarkable: notável
remember: lembrar
remind: trazer à lembrança
renewable: renovável
rephrase: reformular a frase
report: reportar, contar; relatório
research: pesquisar; pesquisa
rest: descansar; resto; descanso
reward: recompensa, prêmio
rice: arroz
ride: cavalgar, andar de
right: direito; certo
ring: tocar; anel
rivalry: rivalidade
river: rio
roast: assar
role: papel; função
roller coaster: montanha--russa
rooftop: telhado
roughly: asperamente, aproximadamente
round: circular; em volta de; redondo
rub: esfregar, friccionar
rudder: leme
rule: regra

sail: velejar
sailor: marinheiro/a
sauce: molho
save: salvar; poupar
score: total de pontos
scramble: esforçar-se para conseguir algo; embaralhar
scratch: arranhar; arranhadura
screen: tela
search: procurar; procura
seasonal: sazonal
seat: assento
sect: seita
seek: procurar; empenhar
seem: parecer
seismic: sísmico; de grandes proporções
self-esteem: autoestima
selfish: egoísta

set: pôr; marcar (uma data)
set up: fundar, estabelecer
settler: colonizador/a
several: vários/as
severe: grave
shake: tremer
shallow: raso/a
shaped: moldado/a
share: dividir, compartilhar
shed: derramar
shelter: abrigo
ship: navio
shirt: camisa
shiver: tremer
shoe: sapato
shot: atirar; tiro
shy: tímido/a
side: lado
signal: indicar, dar indícios; indicação, aviso
silly: bobo/a, estúpido/a
silver: prata; prateado/a
since: desde
single: solteiro/a; único/a
size: tamanho
sizeable: considerável
skill: habilidade, destreza
skim: leitura rápida
skin: pele
skip: saltar, pular
sky: céu
sleigh: trenó
slip: escorregar; escorregão
smelly: fedorento/a
snack: lanche
snail: caracol, lesma
snake: cobra
sneeze: espirrar; espirro
solve: resolver
someone: alguém
something: alguma coisa
soon: em breve
sort: espécie, tipo
soul: alma
spacecraft: nave espacial
spare: sobressalente
spark: faísca
speak out: pronunciar-se
speech: discurso
speed: velocidade
spend: gastar
spicy: condimentado/a, picante
spider: aranha
spilled: derramado/a
spoken: falado/a
spot: mancha
spread: espalhar-se
spring: primavera
squash: queda
squeaky: guinchado/a, rangido/a
squeaky clean: muito limpo/a
stain: manchar; mancha
stair: escada

staple food: alimento principal
start: começar; começo
statement: declaração
stay: ficar, permanecer
steerable: dirigível
stem: caule, haste
step on: pisar em
stirrup: estribo
store: reserva; loja
storyteller: contador/a de histórias
straight out: diretamente de
strength: força
stripped-down: despido/a
strive: aspirar; lutar
strut: peça de madeira ou metal que segura estruturas
stuck: preso/a
stuffing: recheio
stunning: deslumbrante
subject: assunto
such: tal
summer: verão
sum up: resumir
sunny: ensolarado/a
sunscreen: protetor solar
surface: superfície
surgical: cirúrgico/a
survived: sobreviveu
swap: trocar; troca
swear: jurar; xingar
sweat: suar; suor

tag: etiqueta
tail: cauda
take off: decolagem
tale: conto; história
taught: ensinou
tax: imposto; taxa
tea: chá
tear: rasgar; lágrima
tease: provocar, mexer com
teeth: dentes
teller: caixa de banco (funcionário)
tender: afetuoso/a, carinhoso/a
terrific: ótimo/a
than: do que
then: então
thick: espesso/a
thinner: mais magro/a
though: embora
thought: pensamento
through: por meio de
thrust: propulsão, impulso
tickle: fazer cócegas; cócega
tidal: maré
tie: gravata
till: até; até que
tinge: cor, coloração
tiny: pequeno/a

tip-top shape: de bom tamanho
toenail: unha dos dedos dos pés
together: junto, com
tomorrow: amanhã
tongue: língua
tonight: esta noite
too: também; muito, demais
touchdown: pontuação do futebol americano
towards: para (em direção a)
towering: enorme
town: cidade pequena
treat: tratar
trigger: disparar; gatilho
trip: viagem
truth: verdade
try: tentar
tune: melodia
turkey: peru
turn: vez
turn off: desligar
turtle: tartaruga
type: datilografar, digitar

ultimate: último/a, derradeiro/a
ultimately: no fim, por fim
umbrella: guarda-chuva
unaugmented: diminuído/a
unbelievable: inacreditável
uncle: tio
unknown: desconhecido/a
unlikely: improvável
until: até
upcoming: iminente, que está para acontecer
upgrade: melhorar
upon: em cima, acima
upright: ereto/a
upside down: de cabeça para baixo
upward: para cima
utmost: máximo/a

vastly: vastamente
venison: carne de cervo
venom: veneno
venue: local, lugar
vessel: artéria, veia

wacky: maluco/a, engraçado/a
wag: abanar
wagon: vagão de trem
wall: parede; muro

warmth: calor
wave: acenar; onda
wavelength: comprimento de onda
way: jeito; caminho
weak: fraco/a
weakness: fraqueza
weapon: arma
wear: vestir
weather: tempo (atmosférico)
week: semana
weekend: fim de semana
weigh: pesar; peso
welcome: bem-vindo/a
well: bem
wet: molhar; molhado/a
whale: baleia
wheel: roda
wheelchair: cadeira de rodas
wheeler: veículo com rodas
when: quando
whenever: sempre que
where: onde
which: qual
while: enquanto; embora
whilst: enquanto
whitish: esbranquiçado/a
who: quem
whole: inteiro/a, todo/a
whose: de quem; cujo/a
why: por que (em perguntas)
wide: largo/a, amplo/a
widely: amplamente
widespread: generalizado/a
width: largura
wild: selvagem
win: ganhar
wind: vento
wing: asa
wipe: enxugar
wish: desejar, ter vontade; desejo, vontade
within: em, dentro de
wonder: perguntar-se; imaginar
wonderful: maravilhoso/a
worry: preocupar-se; preocupação
worse: pior
worthless: inútil
wrinkle: enrugar, amassar; ruga
wrinkly: enrugado/a
wrist: pulso
wrong: errado/a

yard: quintal
yaw: guinada, correção de rolagem
yawning: enorme

IRREGULAR VERBS

Os verbos podem assumir sentidos diferentes dos listados abaixo, portanto é preciso atentar ao contexto para compreender o significado e o uso de cada um deles.

Base Form	Simple Past	Past Participle	Translation
be	was/were	been	ser; estar
become	became	become	tornar-se
begin	began	begun	começar
buy	bought	bought	comprar
catch	caught	caught	pegar; agarrar
choose	chose	chosen	escolher
come	came	come	vir; chegar
do	did	done	fazer
drink	drank	drunk	beber
drive	drove	driven	dirigir
eat	ate	eaten	comer
fly	flew	flown	voar; pilotar
forget	forgot	forgotten	esquecer
get	got	got/gotten	obter; conseguir; pegar
give	gave	given	dar
go	went	gone	ir
have	had	had	ter
hear	heard	heard	ouvir
know	knew	known	saber; conhecer
let	let	let	deixar; permitir
make	made	made	fazer
say	said	said	dizer
see	saw	seen	ver
send	sent	sent	mandar; enviar
sing	sang	sung	cantar
sleep	slept	slept	dormir
speak	spoke	spoken	falar
swim	swam	swum	nadar
take	took	taken	tomar; pegar; levar
think	thought	thought	pensar
throw	threw	thrown	jogar; lançar
wear	wore	worn	usar; vestir
win	won	won	vencer; ganhar
write	wrote	written	escrever

GRAMMAR HELPER

UNIT 1

Verb to be – Simple Past

O *Simple Past* é usado para tratar de ações que tiveram início e fim em um tempo determinado no passado.

Affirmative	O passado do verbo *to be* é *was/were*	I/He/She	**was**	sick yesterday.
		You/We/You/They	**were**	
		It (the cat)	**was**	sleepy last morning.
Negative	Acrescenta-se *not* ao verbo *to be*. Pode-se também usar as formas contraídas, ou seja, *wasn't* ou *weren't*	I/He/She	**was not (wasn't)**	sick yesterday.
		You/We/You/They	**were not (weren't)**	
		It (the cat)	**was not (wasn't)**	sleepy last morning.
Interrogative	Inverte-se a ordem do verbo *to be* e usa-se a seguinte estrutura: *to be* + sujeito + complemento	**Was**	I/he/she	sick yesterday?
		Were	you/we/you/they	
		Was	it (the cat)	sleepy last morning?

1 Complete the sentences with **was** or **were**.

a. I _____ at home last night. My brothers _____ there, too.

b. He _____ at the beach last weekend.

c. _____ Heather and Ben absent last week?

2 Answer the following questions with information about yourself.

a. Were you on holiday last week? _____

b. Was your sister studying at the same school last year? _____

c. Were your friends with you last weekend? _____

d. Was your cell phone off last night? _____

Past Continuous

O *Past Continuous* descreve uma ação em andamento em algum momento no passado.

Affirmative	sujeito + *to be* no passado (*was/were*) + verbo principal seguido de -*ing*	I/He/She	**was**	read**ing** a book last night.
		You/We/You/They	**were**	
		It	**was**	rain**ing** last night.
Negative	sujeito + *to be* no passado (*was/were*) + *not* + verbo principal seguido de -*ing*	I/He/She	**was not/wasn't**	read**ing** a book last night.
		You/We/You/They	**were not/weren't**	
		It	**was not/wasn't**	rain**ing** last night.
Interrogative	*to be* no passado (*was/were*) + sujeito + verbo principal seguido de -*ing*	**Was**	I/he/she	read**ing** a book last night?
		Were	you/we/you/they	
		Was	it	rain**ing** last night?

3 Complete the sentences with the verbs in parentheses. Use the Past Continuous tense.

a. _____ the tourists _____ for something? They seemed to be lost. (look – interrogative)

b. Carla and I _____ about that new episode. Did you watch it? (talk – affirmative)

c. Richard _____ attention to what the teacher _____. (pay – negative/explain – affirmative)

d. My father _____ dinner when the lights went out. (have – affirmative).

There to be – Simple Past

Para indicar a existência de algo, utiliza-se a forma verbal *there to be*.

Affirmative

A forma afirmativa é composta da seguinte estrutura: *there* + verbo *to be* no passado (*was/were*) + complemento.

| There | was | a person waiting for the bus last night. |
| There | were | people waiting for the bus last night. |

Negative

A forma negativa é composta da seguinte estrutura: *there* + verbo *to be* no passado (*was/were*) + *not* + complemento.

| There | was not/wasn't | a person waiting for the bus last night. |
| There | were not/weren't | people waiting for the bus last night. |

Interrogative

A forma interrogativa é composta da seguinte estrutura: verbo *to be* no passado (*was*/*were*) + *there* + complemento.

Was	there	a person waiting for the bus last night?
Were	there	people waiting for the bus last night?

4 Underline the correct alternative to complete the sentences.

  a. There wasn't/weren't many tickets left to buy. There was/were only four or five!

  b. Was/Were there a movie theater in this neighborhood? Yes, there was/were, but now there are only movie theaters in malls.

  c. Was/Were there cake for her birthday? No, there wasn't/weren't, but there was/were some delicious strawberry cupcakes.

UNIT 2

Simple Past – regular verbs

Affirmative

Para usar a forma afirmativa dos verbos regulares no *Simple Past*, adiciona-se -ed ao verbo principal.

I/He/She/It	
You/We/You/They	liv**ed** across the street from Mike.

Negative

A estrutura usada para indicar a forma negativa é: sujeito + verbo auxiliar *do* no passado (*did*) + *not* + verbo principal. Note que o verbo principal não é conjugado.

I/He/She/It	
You/We/You/They	**did not/didn't live** across the street from Mike.

Interrogative

A forma interrogativa é composta da seguinte estrutura: verbo auxiliar *do* no passado (*did*) + sujeito + verbo principal. O verbo principal permanece inalterado.

Did	I/he/she/it	**live** across the street from Mike?
	you/we/you/they	

1 Complete the sentences with the verbs in parentheses. Use the Simple Past tense.

  a. He _____ the guitar at a concert last week. (play – affirmative)

  b. My parents _____ dinner. We had pizza. (cook – negative)

  c. _____ you _____ during the movie? (cry – interrogative)

Short answers

Para dar respostas curtas, usa-se o verbo auxiliar no passado.

Did you live across the street from Mike?	
Affirmative	Yes, I **did**.
Negative	No, I **didn't**.

UNIT 3

Simple Past – irregular verbs

Os verbos irregulares no passado não têm padrão de conjugação e seguem uma única forma para todos os sujeitos. Na página 166, é possível encontrar uma lista desses verbos, que são exemplificados a seguir.

Infinitive	begin	build	cut	drink	sing	sleep
Simple Past	began	built	cut	drank	sang	slept

Affirmative

Ao usar a forma afirmativa, é importante atentar à forma irregular de cada verbo.

I/He/She/It	**went** to bed late yesterday.
You/We/You/They	

Negative

Para usar a forma negativa, adiciona-se *did + not* (*didn't*). O verbo principal permanece em sua forma básica.

I/He/She/It	**did not/didn't go** to bed late yesterday.
You/We/You/They	

Interrogative

Para usar a forma interrogativa, adiciona-se o verbo auxiliar *did* no início da frase, seguido do sujeito e do verbo principal na forma básica.

Did	I/he/she/it	**go** to bed late yesterday?
	you/we/you/they	

◀1 Complete the sentences with the verbs in parentheses. Use the *Simple Past tense*.

a. I _____ to the park yesterday because I was tired. (go – negative)

b. Last holiday my family _____ to Australia. It was amazing! (go – affirmative)

c. I _____ my friend a secret because I trust him. (tell – affirmative)

2 Write questions in the Simple Past using the information given.

a. you/do your homework/last night

_____

b. you/have a favorite toy/when you were a kid

_____

Past Continuous × Simple Past

O *Past Continuous* expressa uma ação em andamento no passado, e o *Simple Past*, uma ação que já foi concluída.

Usam-se *when* ou *while* para indicar que uma ação no passado estava em andamento quando outra aconteceu ou a interrompeu. Geralmente, usa-se *when* antes do *Simple Past* e *while* antes do *Past Continuous*. Quando duas orações estão no *Past Continuous*, significa que as ações estavam acontecendo ao mesmo tempo no passado; nesse caso, usa-se *while*.

Past Continuous + Simple Past ou vice-versa (**when** or **while**)	I **was listening** to music **when** the mailman **rang** my bell. **When** I **came** back from school, Luiz **was playing** video game. **While** I **was taking** a shower, I **heard** the phone ringing.
Past Continuous + Past Continuous (**while**)	I **was watching** TV **while** my mother **was cooking**.

3 Complete the sentences with **when** or **while**.

a. He wasn't looking at the TV _____ his soccer team scored a goal.

b. My cell phone fell from my hand _____ I was taking a picture.

c. Sharon was cooking lunch _____ her son was washing the dishes.

UNIT 4

Adjective Order

Usados para descrever algo ou alguém, os adjetivos, em geral, vêm antes do substantivo:
The Statue of Liberty is a **beautiful** statue.

Quando há dois ou mais adjetivos, usa-se a seguinte ordem:

The Statue of Liberty is a	opinião	tamanho	idade	formato	cor	origem	material	substantivos
	beautiful	big	old	pointy	green	American	copper	statue.

1 Put the sentences in the correct order using the adjectives in parentheses.

a. My father drives an _____ car. (Russian – old – yellow)

b. This is *ceviche*. It's a _____ typical dish. (delicious – Peruvian)

c. Which one is yours? The _____ one. (metal – new – red)

Comparatives

Os adjetivos também podem ser usados para comparar pessoas ou objetos com o intuito de descrevê-los.

São Paulo is **bigger than** Lisbon.

É importante atentar às regras de escrita dos comparativos.

1. À maioria dos adjetivos de uma sílaba, adicionam-se -er + *than*.
   tall ⟶ My brother is tall**er than** my father.

2. Quando o adjetivo é terminado em -e, adicionam-se apenas -r + *than*.
   large ⟶ Your cell phone is larg**er than** mine.

3. Quando adjetivos de uma sílaba são terminados em vogal + consoante, dobra-se a última consoante e adicionam-se -er + *than*.
   thin ⟶ My mother is thin**ner than** my grandmother.

4. Para adjetivos de duas sílabas terminados em -y, troca-se o -y por -i e adicionam-se -ier + *than*.
   busy ⟶ My friend is bus**ier than** me right now.

5. Para adjetivos longos (com mais de duas sílabas), adicionam-se apenas *more/less* + adjetivo + *than*.
   expensive ⟶ An airplane is **more** expensive **than** a car.

Irregular comparative forms

Alguns adjetivos são irregulares na forma comparativa.

good ⟶ Some cities are **better than** others.

bad ⟶ The book I read last week is **worse than** this one.

far ⟶ My grandparents live **farther/further than** my uncle.

2 Complete the sentences with the correct comparative form. Use the adjectives in parentheses.

a. My best friend is _____ me in basketball. (good)

b. Pepperoni pizza is _____ cheese pizza, don't you think? (delicious)

c. In Brazil, January is usually _____ June. (hot)

Degrees of comparison

Equality

Pode-se comparar pessoas, lugares ou objetos para expressar igualdade. Nesses casos, usa-se a estrutura *as* + adjetivo + *as*.

He is **as intelligent as** his older brother.

Superiority

Pode-se também comparar para expressar superioridade. Nesse caso, para adjetivos curtos, adicionam-se -er + *than*. Já para adjetivos longos, usa-se a estrutura *more* + adjetivo + *than*.

Lisbon is **smaller than** Tokyo.   Tokyo is **more modern than** Lisbon.

Inferiority

Pode-se ainda comparar para expressar inferioridade. Para isso, usam-se as seguintes estruturas: *less* + adjetivo + *than*; *not so/not as* + adjetivo + *as*.

The countryside is **less polluted than** the capital.   The countryside is **not so/as big as** the capital.

3 Complete the sentences using the information in parentheses.

a. Carnival in Bahia is _____ Carnival in Rio de Janeiro.
   (exciting – equality)

b. Mount Rushmore is _____ Mount Everest. (high – inferiority)

c. A motorcycle is _____ a bicycle. (expensive – superiority)

d. Lemons are _____ oranges. (sweet – inferiority)

UNIT 5

Superlatives

Usamos adjetivos superlativos para afirmar que algo ou alguém possui uma qualidade superior em comparação a determinado grupo. Quando usamos o superlativo antes de um substantivo, geralmente ele vem acompanhado do artigo definido *the*.

Veja a seguir a formação dos adjetivos superlativos.

1. Adjetivos curtos em geral: *the* + adjetivo + *-est*.
   old ⟶ **the** old**est** ⟶ I am **the oldest** child in my family.

2. Adjetivos terminados em *-e*: *the* + adjetivo + *-st*.
   close ⟶ **the** clos**est** ⟶ This is **the closest** we can get to the stage.

3. Adjetivos terminados em consoante + vogal + consoante: *the* + adjetivo com a consoante dobrada + *-est*.
   sad ⟶ **the** sad**dest** ⟶ This is **the saddest** movie I have ever watched.

4. Adjetivos terminados em *-y*: substitui-se o *-y* por *-i* e acrescenta-se *-est*.
   easy ⟶ **the** eas**iest** ⟶ I took **the easiest** test of my life last week.

5. Adjetivos longos: *the* + *most* + adjetivo.
   relaxing ⟶ **the most** relaxing ⟶ Yoga is one of **the most relaxing** activities there is.

Irregular superlative forms

Alguns adjetivos são irregulares na forma superlativa.

good → **the best** → Cristiano Ronaldo is one of **the best** soccer players in the world.

bad → **the worst** → The news reported it was **the worst** traffic in the last 10 years today.

far → **the farthest/ the furthest** → Do you know which country is **the farthest** from Brazil?

Inferiority

Para formar adjetivos superlativos que indicam inferioridade, usa-se: *the* + *least* + adjetivo.

famous ⟶ **the least famous** ⟶ He must be **the least famous** vlogger on the internet!

1 Complete the sentences with the correct superlative form. Use the adjectives in parentheses.

a. The cheetah is _____ animal in the world. (fast)

b. If I win the lottery, I will be _____ person in my country! (rich)

c. This must be one of _____ jokes I have ever heard! (funny)

Relative pronouns

Os pronomes relativos são usados para fazer referência a algo já mencionado na frase.

Relative pronoun	Usage	Example
That	Used to refer to things, people, and animals.	The movie **that** won many Oscars this year is a blockbuster.
Which	Used to refer to things and animals.	The movie **which** won many Oscars this year is a blockbuster.
Who	Used to refer to people and pet animals.	The woman **who** is driving fast is going to the hospital.
Whose	Used to indicate possession.	The student **whose** notebook is red is in the restroom.

2 Complete the sentences with the correct *relative pronoun*.

a. The software _____ was installed on the computer last night is not working.

b. The doctor _____ works in this hospital is my uncle.

c. The neighbor _____ dog is very annoying is finally moving out.

UNIT 6

Future – Going to

Para expressar planos ou intenções futuras, usa-se *going to*. Essa estrutura é usada também quando há certeza e/ou evidência de que algo acontecerá.

	subject	verb to be	going to	main verb
Affirmative	I	am	going to	**be** a huge success on TV next year.
	He/She	is		
	You/We/You/They	are		
Negative	subject	verb to be	going to	main verb
	I	am not	going to	**be** a huge success on TV next year.
	He/She	is not/isn't		
	You/We/You/They	are not/aren't		
Interrogative	verb to be	subject	going to	main verb
	Am	I	going to	**be** a huge success on TV next year.
	Is	he/she		
	Are	you/we/you/they		

1 Complete the sentences using **going to** and the information in parentheses.

a. She _____ tonight because she's sick. (study – negative)

b. I _____ some groceries now. (buy – affirmative)

c. _____ you _____ to Jamaica? (travel – interrogative)

d. We _____ a barbecue on Sunday. (have – affirmative)

Reflexive pronouns

Os pronomes reflexivos são usados quando a ação é praticada e sofrida pelo próprio sujeito.

Subject pronoun	Reflexive pronoun	Subject pronoun	Reflexive pronoun
I	myself	it	itself
you	yourself	we	ourselves
he	himself	you	yourselves
she	herself	they	themselves

2 Complete the gaps with the correct *reflexive pronouns*.

a. Tom advised Mary not to go to the park by _____ at night.

b. We taught _____ how to play chess.

c. I baked this chocolate cake _____. Can you believe it?

d. Danny is a big boy already, he can dress by _____.

UNIT 7

Simple Future – Will

O *Simple Future* é usado para fazer previsões, tratar de ações futuras e promessas, falar de um futuro incerto e expressar decisões repentinas.

Affirmative (subject + will + main verb)	I/You/He/She/It/We/You/They	will/'ll	**require** your attention soon.
Negative (subject + will + not + main verb)	I/You/He/She/It/We/You/They	**will + not/ won't**	**be** a difficult matter to solve.
Interrogative (will + subject + main verb)	**Will**	I/you/he/she/it/we/you/they	**start** right now?

1 Complete the sentences with **will**. Use the verbs in parentheses.

a. The phone is ringing. I _____ it right now. (answer – affirmative)

b. I think I _____ my family this summer. I'm too busy. (visit – negative)

c. _____ you _____ to the movies with us tonight? (come – interrogative)

UNIT 8

Prefixes and suffixes

Prefixos e sufixos são adicionados à raiz de uma palavra para mudar seu significado.

Prefix	Meaning	Example
dis-	oposto, desprovido de	**dis**respect
im-/il- in-/ir-	negação, privação	**im**possible
mis-	errado	**mis**place
non-	não	**non**sense
un-	oposto, negação	**un**known
over-	acima de	**over**rated
under-	menos que, abaixo	**under**estimated

Suffix	Meaning	Example
-al	relativo a	colon**ial**
-ful	cheio de	meaning**ful**
-ible	adjetivos	aud**ible**
-ly	advérbios e adjetivos	happ**ily**
-less	destituído de, não afetado por	hope**less**
-y	cheio de (adjetivo)	sunn**y**
-ness	estado ou condição	sick**ness**

◀1 Write down the correct *prefix* or *suffix*.

a. full of hope: _____ (suffix)

b. understand in a wrong way: _____ (prefix)

c. relating to music: _____ (suffix)

d. opposite of agree: _____ (prefix)

Tag questions

As *tag questions* são usadas em final de frase, como forma de confirmar a informação dada. Se a sentença estiver na forma **afirmativa**, a *question tag* ficará na **negativa**. Se a sentença estiver na forma **negativa**, a *question tag* ficará na forma **afirmativa**. Note que as *question tags* apresentam o mesmo tempo verbal e/ou verbo modal da oração principal.

I'**m** not late for class, **am** I?

The dog **is** hungry, **isn't** it?

We **were** very tired last night, **weren't** we?

We **can't leave** this door open, **can** we?

My mother **didn't call** me last night, **did** she?

She **will get** a new cell phone for her birthday, **won't** she?

◀2 Complete the sentences with the correct question tag.

a. This blouse isn't clean,_____

b. We will travel tomorrow at 2:00 p.m, _____

c. Forrest has no idea of what he is doing, _____

d. Andre was sleeping on the couch, _____

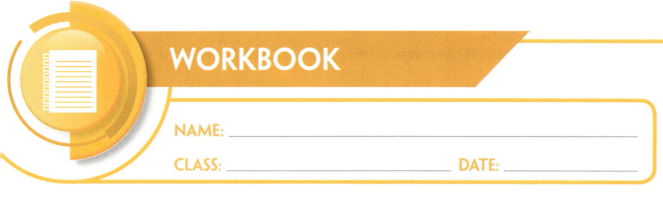

WORKBOOK

NAME: _____

CLASS: _____ DATE: _____

UNIT 1 – ENGLISH: A GLOBAL LANGUAGE

◀ 1   Read the dialog between Jill and Lindsay and match the questions to the answers.

Jill: Hey, Lindsay! Long time no see!

Lindsay: Hi, Jill! I was in South Africa. I arrived yesterday.

Jill: Fantastic! What were you doing there?

Lindsay: I went there to visit my friend Annika. She lives in Cape Town.

Jill: Cool! Is their culture different from ours?

Lindsay: Yes, but they speak English there, too!

Jill: So, you didn't have any problems to communicate, right?

Lindsay: Not really! Some words and expressions in South African English are different from the ones spoken in American English.

Jill: You are kidding me!

Lindsay: For example, we say "barbecue", they say "braai". We say "traffic light", they say "robot". We say "sandwich", they say "sarmie"!

Jill: Wow!

Lindsay: Yes, totally different words!

Jill: Were there many beautiful places to visit?

Lindsay: Yes, there were a lot of them, but the most beautiful was Kirstenbosch National Botanical Garden in Cape Town!

Jill: Would you like to come over to my place so we can talk a bit more about your trip?

Lindsay: Sure! I'm on my way.

David Steele/Shutterstock

a. Where was Lindsay?

b. What was she doing there?

c. What city does Annika live in?

d. Give some examples of South African English words that are different from the ones spoken in American English.

◯ She lives in Cape Town.

◯ Braai, robot, and sarmie.

◯ She was in South Africa.

◯ She went to visit her friend Annika.

2 Complete the questions using **was** or **were**. Then answer them according to the pictures. Follow the example.

a.

_____Was_____ Joanna at school two hours ago?

No, she wasn't. She was at the sports club swimming.

b.

_____ Martin and Frank at the school library yesterday?

_____

c.

_____ mom and dad in the backyard this morning?

_____

d.

_____ Clunkers in my bedroom this afternoon?

_____

3 Complete the sentences using the Past Continuous of the verbs in parentheses.

a. I _____ at the school party last Saturday. I _____ to Michael. (dance – negative/talk)

b. _____ Myrna _____ to school yesterday? No, she _____ calmly. (run/walk)

c. _____ Matt and Fiona _____ to work this morning? No, they _____ to the shopping mall. (go/go)

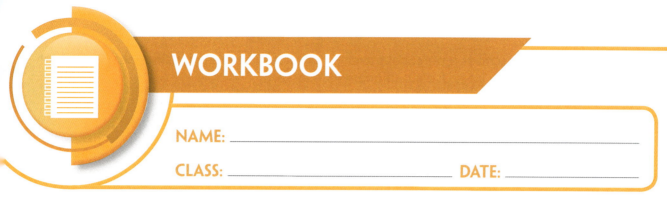

WORKBOOK

NAME: _____

CLASS: _____ DATE: _____

UNIT 2 – HAVING FUN!

1 Read Rachel's e-mail. Then choose two expressions from the box to complete it.

be a wet blanket   be the life and soul of the party   be a shrinking violet

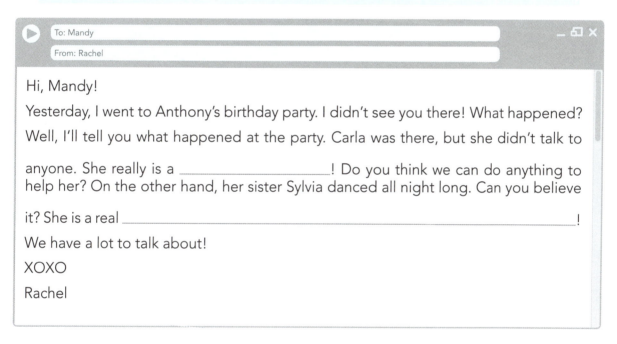

To: Mandy
From: Rachel

Hi, Mandy!

Yesterday, I went to Anthony's birthday party. I didn't see you there! What happened?

Well, I'll tell you what happened at the party. Carla was there, but she didn't talk to

anyone. She really is a _____! Do you think we can do anything to help her? On the other hand, her sister Sylvia danced all night long. Can you believe

it? She is a real _____!

We have a lot to talk about!

XOXO

Rachel

2 Imagine you are Mandy. Write an e-mail to Rachel explaining why you didn't go to Anthony's party. Ask her more questions about the event.

To: Rachel
From: Mandy

3 The text below describes a personal travel experience. Complete it using the Simple Past of the verbs from the box. Use a dictionary if necessary.

be	cross	invite	post	travel

www.letmestayforaday.com/

"My name is Ramon Stoppelenburg. When I _____ 24, I left my house in The Netherlands, on May 1, 2001, with a backpack full of clothing, a digital camera, a laptop, and a mobile phone. From May 2001 to July 2003,

I _____ the world without any money, visiting people who

_____ me over through this website. I _____ distance with my thumb or with help of sponsors and supporters. In return for the

support, I _____ my personal travel experiences in my daily reports on this website."

Based on: <www.letmestayforaday.com/>. Accessed on: Mar. 19, 2019.

4 Read Ramon Stoppelenburg's personal travel experience again and answer the questions.

a. What did he decide to do when he was 24 years old?

_____

_____

b. What did he do from May 2001 to July 2003?

_____

_____

c. How did Ramon cross distance?

_____

_____

d. Did he write daily reports? Why (not)?

_____

_____

5 If you could ask Ramon two questions, what would you ask him?

_____

_____

_____

_____

WORKBOOK

NAME: _____

CLASS: _____ DATE: _____

UNIT 3 – REMARKABLE PEOPLE

1 Read the fragments below about three remarkable women and guess who they are. Then circle their occupations. Use a dictionary if necessary.

a. She (born Stefani Joanne Angelina Germanotta) is an American songwriter, singer, actress, philanthropist, dancer, and fashion designer.

Based on: <www.imdb.com/name/nm3078932/bio>. Accessed on: Mar. 16, 2019.

_____

b. She (born July 6, 1907, Coyoacán, Mexico—died July 13, 1954, Coyoacán) was a Mexican painter best known for her uncompromising and brilliantly coloured self-portraits that deal with such themes as identity, the human body, and death.

Based on: <https://corporate.britannica.com/>. Accessed on: Mar. 16, 2019.

_____

c. She (15 April 1990) is a British actress and social activist. She rose to prominence through her role as Hermione in the Harry Potter film series. In recent years, she has been a spokesperson on women's rights and other social issues.

Based on: <www.biographyonline.net/people.html>. Accessed on: Mar. 16, 2019.

_____

2 Now label the pictures below with the names of the women from activity 1. There is one extra picture. Who is this person and what is she famous for?

a.

_____

b.

_____

c.

_____

d.

_____

3 Complete the dialog below using the verbs from the box in the Simple Past. You can use them more than once.

> be   die   disappear   fly   have

Joshua: What a boring day, Marla!

Marla: What about playing a guessing game, Joshua? I think of a remarkable person and you try to guess who he/she is. I will give you a clue: she _____ born in 1897.

Joshua: When _____ she _____ ?

Marla: Probably in 1937.

Joshua: Probably? _____ she _____?

Marla: Yes, she _____ in 1937.

Joshua: _____ she _____ an accident?

Marla: Yes!

Joshua: _____ she a pilot?

Marla: Yes, she _____! What's her name?

Pictorial Press Ltd/Alamy/Fotoarena

Joshua: Amelia Earhart! She _____ the first female pilot that _____ across the Atlantic Ocean! She _____ several notable flights. Your turn, Marla!

4 Complete the sentences below with the verbs in parentheses in the correct tense.

a. Dad _____ home when mom arrived from New York. (drive)

b. The earthquake _____ when people were sleeping. (begin)

c. While we were preparing the surprise party, Patricia _____ in! (come)

d. The telephone _____ when they were having breakfast. (ring)

5 Join the fragments and, in your notebook, write sentences using **some** or **any**.

I. He doesn't have	• paper in the computer lab today.
II. Students can't write	• idea about what happened yesterday.
III. Carla bought	• new clothes at the mall.

UNIT 4 – COMPARING FACTS AND SCENES

1 Choose some adjectives to describe the pictures below and classify them according to what they express: opinion, size, age, shape, color, or origin.

	a	b	c	d
opinion				
size				
age				
shape				
color				
origin				

Carro vermelho: VanderWolf Images/Shutterstock; Filme da Disney: WALT DISNEY PRODUCTIONS/Album/Fotoarena; Carro antigo: Wolfiser/Shutterstock; Guepardo: rokopix/Shutterstock

2 Check the correct order of adjectives to complete the sentences.

a. Donald has two _____ cats. Their names are Sissy and Pam.

○ beautiful, small, black   ○ black, beautiful, small

b. My mother brought from Europe a _____ clock.

○ wonderful, old, Italian   ○ old, wonderful, Italian

c. Please, can you reach that _____ box for me?

○ yellow, big, square   ○ big, square, yellow

d. The Carters went to an _____ cruise last month.

○ incredible, huge, brand-new, Caribbean   ○ incredible, Caribbean, huge, brand-new

3 Complete the text below using the adjectives from the box. You can use them more than once and in the comparative form.

| attentive | funny | nice | patient | talkative |

www.helloteens.com

Hi, Jack!

Today was my first day at Saint Paul's School. Guess who are in my class? The

triplets Angelica, Tina, and Nelson! Well, Angelica is a _____ girl, but Tina

is _____ and _____. Nelson is _____ _____

_____ his sisters. He can't stop talking! They were happy to see me there!

The Math teacher seems to be _____ _____ _____ Ms.
Anderson, she doesn't like to explain things twice. But my new English teacher is

_____ _____ to students _____ Ms. Allison. Ms. Thompson is so
helpful and polite!

Well, come over to my place so we can talk about my new school!

See you!

Banco de imagens/Arquivo da editora

4 Observe and read the cartoon below. Then complete it using the comparative form of the adjective **pretty**.

GLASBERGEN
© Randy Glasbergen
glasbergen.com

© Randy Glasbergen Cartoon/Acervo do cartunista

"**Don't be silly...you're** *much* _____ **than anyone I dated before you!**"

WORKBOOK

NAME: _____

CLASS: _____ DATE: _____

UNIT 5 – THE AMAZING HUMAN BODY

1 Read the text below, underline the correct options to complete it, and write them in the correct place.

The Most Important Organ In Your Body

I have a question for everybody reading this. What is (1) _____ organ in the human body? Many of you are probably thinking it is the heart. While your heart is a vital organ, the brain and of course the nervous system that attaches to

your (2) _____ make up (3) _____ organ system in the human body.

The human nervous system is responsible for coordinating every movement or action your body takes. The nervous system is responsible for every function of the human body. In order for your

(4) _____ to beat, your (5) _____ to breath and your (6) _____ to walk your nervous system has to be functioning properly.

If your nervous system is out of whack you likely have a lot of health problems. [...]

Available at: <http://spinealignchiropractic.com/health/important-organ-body/>.Accessed on: Mar. 16, 2019.

(1) **the most important/the best**	(3) **the most critical/the biggest**	(5) **bones/lungs**
(2) **skin/brain**	(4) **heart/liver**	(6) **feet/femur**

2 Label the organs below and match them to some of their functions.

a.
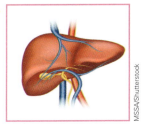

b.
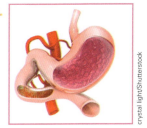

c.
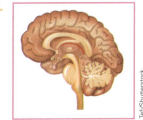

_____   _____   _____

Based on: <www.webmd.com>. Accessed on: Mar. 16, 2019.

3 Check the correct alternative to complete the sentences and write the answers in the blank spaces.

a. Even with _____ healthcare system, yellow fever can reach Europe.

○ the best   ○ the worst

b. **A:** *A Star is Born* is _____ movie of the year. It's so boring!

B: Are you nuts? It's _____ movie ever!

○ the funniest/the saddest   ○ the least interesting/the greatest

c. **A:** In my opinion, Sandra is _____ Sophie. She always scores A in her school tests.

B: That's true, but her sister is _____ in the classroom. She makes me laugh all the time!

○ the most intelligent/funnier   ○ more intelligent than/the funniest

4 The sentences below are not complete. Choose the correct endings from the box and use relative pronouns to join both fragments.

> is trained in the art of building design.
> passport was stolen?
> received a lung transplant last month.
> were in the fridge?

a. Where are the carrots _____

b. An architect is someone _____

c. What is the name of the girl _____

d. That is the patient _____

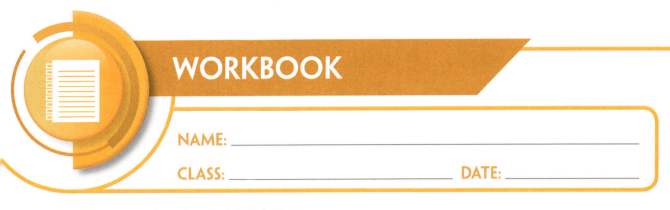

WORKBOOK

NAME: _____

CLASS: _____ DATE: _____

UNIT 6 – DIGITAL WORLD

1 Read the dialog below and complete it using the expressions from the box. Then answer the questions.

> enter chat rooms   post videos and photos

Jack: Hi, Steve! Are you OK?

Steve: No, I'm upset! My mom told me off and took my smartphone! She said that I spend too much time on the internet.

Jack: How long do you spend on the internet every day, Steve?

Steve: About eight hours...

Jack: What do you do on the internet for so many hours?

Steve: Well, I _____ . Sometimes I _____ because I like to make new online friends.

Jack: Hey, buddy, this is dangerous! I'm sorry, but your mother is right.

a. Do you agree with Jack? Why (not)?

_____

_____

_____

b. What would you say to Steve about his situation?

_____

_____

_____

c. How many hours do you spend on the internet every day? What do you usually do online?

_____

_____

_____

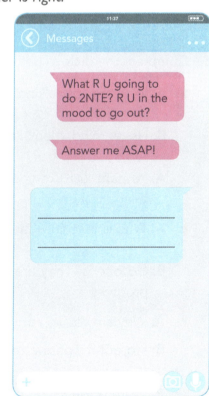

2 Read the instant message and answer it using IM language.

3 Read the questions below and answer them using the clues given and **going to**.

a. Did you wash the car this morning, Chris?

Not yet. _____. (tomorrow)

b. Did your brother repair your laptop?

Not yet. _____. (in a few minutes)

c. Did Sue post photos of her marriage yesterday?

Not yet. _____. (tonight)

d. Did the kids finish their house chores?

Not yet. _____. (later)

4 What do you think is going to happen in the following situations? Read the sentences, think about their context, and answer them.

a. The sky is full of dark clouds and thunders. It _____.

b. Mark is still sleeping and it's 11:00 a.m.! His test starts in 20 minutes!

He _____.

c. Sue was not invited to Ann's birthday party and they are classmates!

Sue _____.

5 Complete the dialogs below using the correct reflexive pronouns.

a. **A:** Who are you talking to, my dear?

B: Never mind, mom. I'm talking to _____.

A: You are just like your father! He always talks to _____ when he is taking a shower!

b. **A:** Who is teaching Carlo and Vanessa how to develop web pages?

B: No one is. They are teaching _____, but they are not making any progress.

c. **A:** Why are you so angry, Daniel?

B: I forgot my password and I can't access my online messages.

A: Calm down and control _____!

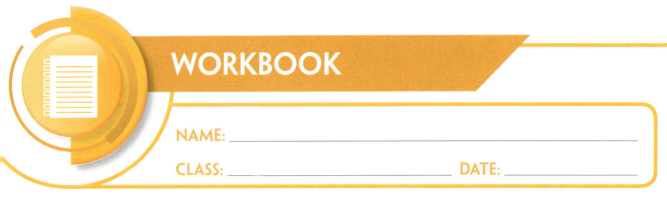

NAME: _____

CLASS: _____ DATE: _____

UNIT 7 – LIGHTS, CAMERA, ACTION!

1 Complete the gaps with the appropriate movie genre and the expressions from the box.

> dramas   futuristic technology   portraying realistic characters   action
>
> spectacular rhythm   sci-fi   life situations   visionary and imaginative

---

www.filmsite.org/genres.html   _ ⊡ ×

Main Film Genres

_____ films usually include high energy, big-budget physical stunts and chases, possibly with rescues, battles, fights, escapes, destructive crises (floods, explosions, natural disasters, fires etc.), non-stop motion,

_____ and pacing, and adventurous, often two-dimensional 'good-guy' heroes (or recently, heroines) battling 'bad guys' [...].

_____ are serious, plot-driven presentations,

_____, settings, _____, and stories involving intense character development and interaction. [...]

_____ films are often quasi-scientific,

_____ – complete with heroes, aliens, distant planets, impossible quests, improbable settings, fantastic places, great dark and

shadowy villains, _____, unknown and unknowable forces, and extraordinary monsters ('things or creatures from space'), either created by mad scientists or by nuclear havoc. [...]

Available at: <www.filmsite.org/genres.html>. Accessed on: Mar. 16, 2019.

2 Imagine you and your friend are planning to watch a movie next weekend. Read the questions and answer them properly to create a dialog.

Your friend: What will you do next weekend?

You: _____

Your friend: What about watching a movie?

You: _____

Your friend: Well, I love sci-fi and action movies! What about you?

You: _____

Your friend: So, let's choose the movie... Any suggestions?

You: _____

Your friend: Awesome!

3 Complete the following sentences using the Simple Future with **will**.

a. **A:** Can you call me later, mom?

   B: Sure, I _____ tonight.

b. **A:** Can you help me repair my laptop keyboard, Carl?

   B: Yes. I'm busy now, but I _____ tomorrow, OK?

c. **A:** Can you take the kids to the movies, honey?

   B: Of course! I _____ next weekend.

d. **A:** Don't tell anyone the end of the movie! No spoilers, Adam, please!

   B: OK. I _____ how the movie ends.

4 Write questions and answers according to the clues in parentheses.

a. Why/turn the TV on? (to be)
   We/watch *A Star Is Born.* (to go)

   _____

   _____

b. Which cities/visit next month? (will)
   I/visit Rome, Venice and Milan. (will)

   _____

   _____

5 What would you do in the situations below?

a. **A:** Oh, my God! I don't have any money with me!

   B: I _____.

b. **A:** Are we going to the movies tonight? You know, I love watching movies!

   B: No, we aren't. We _____.

WORKBOOK

NAME: _____

CLASS: _____ DATE: _____

UNIT 8 – LET'S CELEBRATE!

1 Read about an important Brazilian festivity and check the correct options to complete the text.

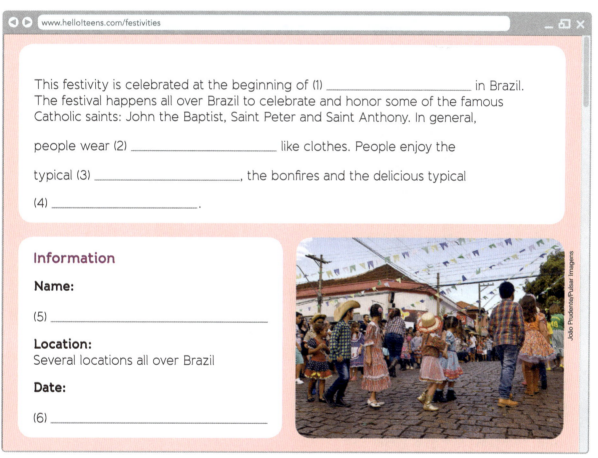

www.hello!teens.com/festivities

This festivity is celebrated at the beginning of (1) _____ in Brazil. The festival happens all over Brazil to celebrate and honor some of the famous Catholic saints: John the Baptist, Saint Peter and Saint Anthony. In general,

people wear (2) _____ like clothes. People enjoy the

typical (3) _____, the bonfires and the delicious typical

(4) _____ .

Information

Name:

(5) _____

Location:
Several locations all over Brazil

Date:

(6) _____

João Prudente/Pulsar Imagens

Based on: <http://trip-n-travel.com/listicle/21758/>. Accessed on: Mar. 16, 2019.

	(1)	(2)	(3)	(4)	(5)	(6)
Festa Junina						
mid June-August						
food						
farmers						
dances						
winter						

2 Underline the correct tag question in each of the sentences below.

a. You don't know when does Lavagem do Bonfim happen, **do I?/do you?**

b. It's 9:00 o'clock now. Tom will be late to work again, **won't he?/will it?**

c. The kids wouldn't like to stay indoors the whole day, **would they?/wouldn't they?**

d. Carol doesn't want to go to work on foot anymore, **does she?/does Carol?**

e. Jason and his brother had enough money to visit Salvador last year, **didn't they?/ didn't them?**

3 Complete the dialog with the words from the box.

he	her	his	mine	our
ours	she	they	we	yours

Claire: John, hurry up! _____ are going to miss _____ plane!

John: Calm down, Claire. Is this bag _____?

Claire: Of course not! The gray one is _____. Maybe it's Lisa's.

Lisa: No, it's Paul's. _____ leaves his bag anywhere! It's _____, for sure!

Paul: Come on, Lisa! Mom, _____ never knows where _____ things are!

Claire: _____ two, stop now! Whose passports are these?

Lisa and Paul: _____ are _____, mom. Sorry...

John: So, let's go. Carnival in Rio awaits us!

Jupiterimages/Getty Images